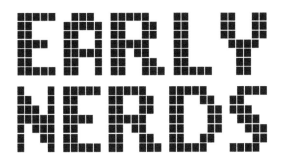

EARLY NERDS

Almost-True Stories from Silicon Valley

Steve Rubin

R.L. Ranch Press

Greenville, South Carolina

Early Nerds

Acknowledgments

A special thanks to Amy Lansky, my wife, lover, collaborator, and best friend forever. My two sons, Izaak and Max, always have great comments as well. I couldn't have done this without such a supportive family.

Thanks also to my editor, Jena Roach, who continues to push me to do better, and to Diogo Leite of Book Design Company for a simple but catchy cover.

I was motivated to write these stories by the works of Damon Runyon, who wrote about the gamblers, gangsters, and other lowlife denizens of New York City in the early 1900s. I have even borrowed his format, writing in first-person, present tense, yet making the narrator a nameless member of the group who rarely experiences the action himself and instead relies on stories told by others. I've avoided Runyon's stylized language, but I've kept one significant aspect of all his pieces: the twist ending. So a major acknowledgment goes to Damon Runyon, whose clever tales have inspired me more than somewhat.

Finally, thanks go to the many nerds I have known in a long computing career. If you know me, you may find yourself here, and if you do, or if you find characters with traits that seem awfully familiar, all I can say is, you're welcome.

Table of Contents

To all the early computer nerds ...
you know who you are.

The Library

Big corporations are falling all over themselves to figure out how they can make a buck from these new piles of wires that are called a computer. Regardless of whether the company makes appliances, ambulances, or airplanes, they've got research labs to explore this mostly unknown field. Anyone with a dollop of computer literacy has a job waiting, and those with deeper skills are elevated from their once-shamed awkwardness to sudden heights of respect. It's revenge of the nerds, hard core.

I've recently started work in a lab run by Pavel Foote, a tall thin man who all the nerds quickly dub Uncle Pavel, because like a mythical rich uncle, he showers us with much goodness. He invites us to his home for a welcome party after the lab is formed, and it's immediately obvious that the goodness he sprinkles on us rains more heavily on himself. His spacious home has stunning views of Silicon Valley and its promise of prosperity. From his deck, we can see the Spanish tile roofs of Stanford University nestled in the trees, as well as the airport and some bay bridges, all connected by a network of highways beneath the faint yellow haze of auto smog. This is the life.

With a wide grin spanning his narrow face, Uncle Pavel gives a tour of his house, emphasizing the structural elements in the building, the ultramodern heating system, the clever way the panoramic glass panels are attached, and the sophisticated pier system that supports the structure on the side of the mountain. It's a typical nerd response to such a space, talking more about unobserved details instead of mentioning, even once, that the views are breathtaking. And Uncle Pavel is, like all of us, a nerd.

After so much architectural talk, it comes as no surprise that Uncle Pavel is a woodworker. He shows us the fine furniture he's built, each piece carefully constructed from rare and thoughtfully considered lumber. His work is fascinating, with colorful inlaid triangles forming dazzling patterns around perfectly finished surfaces. He even shows us his woodshop, a former garage now filled with large power tools and cabinets full of hand tools, many of obscure Japanese provenance that sport bamboo handles and deadly sharp edges. He boasts that when he's done with a woodworking session, it takes him an extra hour to clean and oil the metal, then store each tool comfortably in its own cloth bag to protect it from the threat of rust. I am impressed.

At the party, I get to know a few of the others in the lab, including a massive fellow named Robin King who's as big as any two normal computer nerds. Around the lab, he's already been dubbed The Mountain because of his Paul Bunyan build and his lumberjack work clothes. He even likes to go hunting and occasionally reports spending the weekend digging holes for fence posts up at his mountain spread. Most of us who fall in love with computers do so because we're bad at digging holes.

The Mountain's wife is Charlie Jackson, who works in another research lab. Charlie is intense and serious with quick robotic speech patterns that are unemotional and direct. She's easily as tall as The Mountain, but unlike him, is the size of only one computer nerd. Charlie tells me about the spread they recently bought with plenty of land, a barn, and a small house. They have grand plans for a larger home as well as fields of crops and many animals. I'm exhausted just hearing about it. Of all the nerds I've met, these two are the heartiest.

A man shows up at the party who seems thoroughly out of place. He's average looking in all respects except that he's wearing a three-piece suit which surprises me, since none of us—not even Uncle Pavel—ever dress that way, neither at parties nor at work. Here in Silicon Valley, those who wear a suit are either lost or seeking a job. Uncle Pavel introduces him as Thomas Meridian, the site manager responsible for all the buildings at work, including many groups not related to our lab. Given his proper attire, I'm hardly surprised he speaks with a posh British accent. He quickly makes some introductions then leaves to let the party finish on its own.

But over the next few months, I see Thomas more and more. He often drops computer terms into his conversations, so at first I think he knows something. But as I experience more of his wisdom, I realize there is none, at least as far as computers go. He simply likes to talk that way. We generally ignore him, and nobody suggests a nickname, except to add unpleasant epithets that fail to amuse or stick. He's just Thomas, and that's as much as any of us want to know when interacting with the man.

Thomas has a disquieting habit of using pleasant expressions when he is not at all pleased. I overhear an interchange between him and Uncle Pavel when I pass the two of them in the hall one day. Uncle Pavel is hoping to hire six more people, but Thomas grumbles, "Sorry, but you're only getting three, *my friend.*" Uncle Pavel grimaces, then replies, "Yes, *sir.*" It's a chilling lesson in double-speak, because Thomas's "friend" implies that Uncle Pavel is anything but; and our boss's derisive "sir," really means, "you contemptible asshole."

Thomas comes to our weekly meeting one day, which immediately makes people start to fidget. As soon as he walks in the door, I see enough subtle facial expressions to do a vaudeville act. What bad news is he going to deliver now? He waits for everyone to get seated, then he clears his throat. "OK, listen up, people." His opening salvo causes an eruption of twitches that flows in a wave around the table. He leans closer and lowers his voice. "You've got too many books, and something must be done."

There's no denying the truth here. Each of us has our own private collection of papers, journals, lab notes, printouts, conference proceedings, and yes, books. But the lab has a more extensive collection, and it's been sitting in boxes that line the hallways. This makes them rather unusable and a source of frustration for those desperate enough to need something and brave enough to search. Uncle Pavel has tried to get more space for these books, and since the subject has been broached, he pushes once again for a library that could make life so much easier. All of us quietly nod our assent to this idea, just in case the dreaded site-manager thinks he can get away with an alternate solution.

Thomas sees that we're in agreement, but he's come prepared and acquiesces in a rather bizarre way. We can have our library, he tells us, if we build it ourselves. There are a few large and unused storage sheds along the side of the building, which are no good for books because they're unheated and not sealed well enough. But he's willing to remove two of them, leaving us with a decent-sized concrete pad to construct a better space. There's even an outside door near the two sheds, which will become the entrance to our new library. All we need to do is get it built, and he's willing to pay for the materials. But it's up to us to find someone who can do the work, which means it will be paid from the lab's budget. With his best offer on the table, Thomas leaves the room.

As soon as he's gone, Uncle Pavel gives us a vigorous fist pump. "This is great news, boys and girls. I'm going to build this one myself." Given Uncle Pavel's woodworking skills, he does seem like the person for the job. Of course, considering his devotion to fine woodworking, our library will look like a museum when he's done, but that's not a problem.

At the other end of the room, however, The Mountain pounds the table. "No, no, and no. If we wait for you to engrave detail into every corner, we'll never have a library. Let's get some people who know construction. Charlie and I are building a new home up on Skyline, so we can have the library done much sooner."

Stunned by this rejection, Uncle Pavel insists he can do the job at the appropriate level of workmanship and in a reasonable amount of time. The Mountain remains unconvinced, and from what I know of the situation, he may be right. The discussion goes on for most of the meeting, Uncle Pavel asserting he can do this, while The Mountain maintaining that he cannot and should not. It seems to me that I must either intervene or leave, and leaving the weekly group meeting is very unfriendly, so I speak up.

"If you both think you can build it quickly, let's make a competition." I now have everyone's attention. "Let's build a two-room library. Uncle Pavel can build one room, and The Mountain can find someone to build the other. The first to finish wins."

Uncle Pavel thinks for a few seconds before pushing back. "There will be a common wall separating the rooms. Who will build that?"

I shrug. "How about this? The first one to get that far has to build the common wall. It will handicap that person, forcing them to do extra work, and it will give the other person time to catch up. You two will have to discuss your plans to get the dimensions right, but I'm sure it can be worked out."

Silence blankets the room as the two contestants think this over. Uncle Pavel looks ready to agree, but he has a few more concerns. "So who are you going to get to build your half?"

The Mountain laughs. "Oh, just me and Charlie. We've been planning to do an addition to our new house, so we'll practice on the library. Plus, we'll do it for free, which will save the lab some money."

"You?" Uncle Pavel's voice drips with derision. "You've never built anything in your life. You may be able to hunt and ride a horse, but I wouldn't want to put my books in a library that you built. It's going to fall apart as soon as you finish it. Hell, do you even have any tools? I have an entire workshop."

"Eh." The Mountain casually flips a hand. "I've got a few tools. Figure I'll get a few more and we're ready to work. Trust me, this will be solid."

But Uncle Pavel is not ready to trust. "We can't have a crappy library. If you don't build it right, it's going to cost extra to pull it down and start over."

"Oh, come on! If I can't do it right, *I'll* be the one to pull it down. I'm not asking for money, so you haven't got anything to lose. Besides, Unk, we need this and fast. So let's work together."

Uncle Pavel pauses before flashing a subtle smile. "OK, you're on." Then he exposes a part of himself that shows why he's the lab director. "Let's make it more interesting. Put a side bet on this. Whoever builds their room first gets something from the other."

The Mountain leans closer, clearly unafraid to play. "What do you want from me if I lose?"

Uncle Pavel already has an answer. "If you lose, you have to give me your pickup truck. I've been looking for one, but I'll take yours. What do you say?" He folds his arms, daring The Mountain to sacrifice his precious vehicle.

But The Mountain only laughs harder. "OK, but if you lose, I get your TR7."

A collective gasp sucks the air from the room. Uncle Pavel's Triumph TR7 is an expensive little sports car, worth more than any pickup truck. This bet is wildly unfair. But Uncle Pavel suffers from a serious abundance of ego, and he apparently sees no way of losing the bet, so he offers his hand in agreement, and the two of them shake. The race is on.

Thomas keeps his promise, and by the next day, the sheds are removed. I'm outside examining the weathered concrete floor, dubious that they can ever house our delicate pieces of paper. But The Mountain is already pacing it out, taking measurements and making notes of the remaining bolts and brackets, all of them looking far from new. Uncle Pavel shows up and they discuss dimensions. It's a sorry conversation. Each time The Mountain mentions something he intends to do, Uncle Pavel sneers and explains why it's wrong. The discussion isn't going well for The Mountain, who is sadly out of his element, losing nearly every point he makes.

After some deliberation, Uncle Pavel departs to his office, but The Mountain gets in his pickup truck, perhaps to savor it one last time before he's forced to hand the keys to his boss. As he's about to drive away, he motions me over. "Get in. We're going shopping."

I can't help The Mountain build this, but he needs assistance loading the truck, and as the nearest warm body, I'm elected. We head to a lumber yard in Mountain View, and when he arrives, he calls Charlie to describe the task he's undertaken. They talk at length, discussing lumber and tool requirements, and I depart to wander the cavernous warehouse stacked so high with wood it feels like an entire forest died here. It even smells like a forest, with fresh cut lumber moving past me on beeping forklifts.

The Mountain returns from his phone call with a cocky swagger and a rolling cart. He starts to shop, and we fill the cart as well as a few others with endless board-feet of wood, a variety of roofing materials, and even a window. He's confident, but I am much less so, having no idea how he intends to win this bet against the vastly more experienced Uncle Pavel.

After two hours of shopping, The Mountain nearly maxes out his credit card on a truckload of supplies. He even buys a nail gun, which makes sense to me, but what about a saw? Is he going to cut this wood by hand? Paul Bunyan could do it, but The Mountain will need tools. I ask him about this a number of times, but he assures me he knows what he's doing and will have no trouble, especially if Charlie helps. With an extra ton thunking in back, we return to the lab and unload, then he departs for home.

I get comfortable at my computer, which is far easier for me to comprehend than building supplies. Soon I'm lost in the work and fully detached from this silly bet. It could be months before we have even one room of the library, and I wonder if I made a mistake by proposing a competition.

The next morning, when I come to the office, The Mountain is outside the main door, as is Charlie. They're sitting in folding lawn chairs, talking and laughing together, sharing a steaming thermos of coffee. When they see me, they jump up and beckon me to the side of the building. There, in the morning light, is the entire library building, both rooms, with walls, a window, and a mostly shingled roof. If my eyebrows could arch any higher, they'd leap off my face.

"You two built the whole library last night?"

The Mountain snickers and gives his wife a hug. "Teamwork. It was easy." He gestures around the building, now littered with scrap wood, roofing detritus, ladders, and a tripod-mounted light. These two have been busy.

We return to the front and enter the main building, then use the side door which is now our library's entrance. The interior is unfinished, so the walls are exposed, ready for ducts and electrical work. But the basic structure is complete, which baffles me.

I give Charlie and The Mountain a look of confused wonder. "How did you do this?"

Before The Mountain can answer, Uncle Pavel arrives and his jaw clangs hard on the floor. "This isn't possible!" He runs his hand over the wall, then he huffs loudly. "Crude. Look at how rough this wood is." At another place he shakes his head like a disappointed teacher. "This edge isn't even straight."

The Mountain rolls his eyes. "Well, what did you expect? I haven't got the hundreds of fine tools you have. I have only one saw, so I cut everything by hand. The lines may not be perfect, but it's solid. Look at these posts and beams." He slams his palm against a corner post, eliciting barely a thud as the wood refuses to move.

Our lab director is even more annoyed. "You're supposed to use four-by-fours here, not eight-by-eights. This post is way too big."

"Yeah," The Mountain gives a loud whoop. "This building isn't going anywhere. And don't worry about the irregular edges. I bought trim to cover them, so it'll be as pretty as you like."

Uncle Pavel keeps running his hand over the wood, all of it rough as bark. He considers the scattered tools and points to the nail gun. "OK, I see you nailed it together with this, but how did you cut the wood? You say you cut everything by hand, and from these sloppy edges, I can tell. But you must have used a power tool to get this done so quickly." He looks around, muttering to himself. "Hmm, no radial arm saw. No table saw. A circular saw can't cut those huge posts. What the hell?" He throws his hands in the air. "I give up. What kind of saw do you have, and how did one person do this so fast?"

The Mountain is mid-yawn, still recovering from his all-nighter and trying to ignore Uncle Pavel's lecture, but this last comment snaps him to attention. "One person, eh? There are two of us, Unk, or didn't you notice?" He wraps an arm around his wife. "And here's something you probably don't know. Before Charlie became a programmer, she worked as a carpenter. She knows all about construction, so she might have used one of those saws you mentioned. But I have a different way of cutting wood that I really enjoy. Let me show you."

He leads us back outside, ducks into a corner of the building, and returns with a massive chain saw, able to fell big trees with ease. It looks normal in his hands, which means it would be a monstrously oversized tool for anyone else. With a grunt, The Mountain pulls the cord to fire up the engine. Nasty looking teeth spin dangerously as he revs the motor, and he snarls as he waves his favorite toy at Uncle Pavel.

"Your car keys, please."

Bikes

Red-Ink Vlad arrives at work in full leather, a motorcycle helmet clutched under an arm and his few remaining strands of hair sweat-glued to his scalp. Vlad is not a young man, but he still rides on two wheels whenever possible and claims to own four of these beasts. I'd gladly trade four motorcycles for two automobiles, which would have the same number of tires but be much more comfortable. Even Vlad agrees that he's getting a little old for this foolishness, but he can't resist the road.

"You're back!" I realize I haven't seen him all week and it's late Friday afternoon.

"Yeah." He struggles with his jacket sleeve, peeling more leather off his tall solid body. "Just got in from Reno. Need a shower." He pauses with an upward stare, perhaps replaying a vista or some roadside thrill, a millimeter of a smile on his face. Then he nods and walks down the hall.

His name is Vladimir MacKenzie, but we call him Red-Ink Vlad because as the most senior scientist in our lab, who's penned many technical articles and books, we bring our papers to him for comment. Then he "bleeds red ink," as he likes to say, scribbling voluminous notes with his trusty red pen. Our papers come back with a full range of comments, catching everything from spelling errors and awkward sentences to whole-work criticisms and suggestions for further research. It's not easy to get comments from Vlad, but it's always worthwhile.

Red-Ink Vlad isn't the only person in the lab who rides a motorcycle. Andy Jones, who we like to call Big Andy, has two of them. Our official lab athlete, he's ruggedly built, has an eternally twisted grin, and loves extreme sports.

Another chopper nerd is Give Me All What We Have, whose nickname is tiresomely long but always worth saying. His name is Broderick Borui-Xiaoling, an average-size but muscular nerd with a passion for playing ice hockey. He got his nickname from a student programmer who created an annoying computer system that would show your data only after you typed the command, "give me all what we have." Estavio was so baffled by this preposterous command that he stopped saying, "hello" when he met people and instead demanded, "Give me all what we have." The nickname may be long, but it's still fewer syllables than his full name.

And if there aren't enough nerds with bikes, the two Canadians in our lab—Iggy and Boom—each ride and own a handful of motorcycles. That's five hard-core nerds I know, just in this one small lab, who not only ride but probably own a dozen motorcycles between them. It almost makes me want to try it. Almost.

Now the average nerd does not ride a bike and will offer medical statistics to prove that riding is a foolish way to travel. Given this, I'm endlessly amused by all the talk I hear in the lab. The riders take biking vacations in the Southern California desert where they raise clouds of sandy dust, then sit around the campfire to play music and get high. Or perhaps they get high first, then raise clouds of dust and play music; even they are never sure. And since they're bikers, there must also be plenty of alcohol. They return from these trips with stories that hardly seem true.

One claim is certainly true about these trips: the music. Iggy and Boom are the guitarist and bass players in our lab's band, The Dead Snails. They played together back in Alberta, and now they're here, making noise for everyone. The Dead Snails also features Standard on vocals and Wings on drums. Standard is Stanley Ardman, tall and thin, with shoulder-length brown hair that he keeps in a pony tail and only occasionally lets down. Wings is Cyril Polivka, an intense and stocky Czechoslovakian who hang glides. He has dark unkempt hair, a thick mustache, and two PhDs, one from each side of the Iron Curtain.

Even though Boom rides motorcycles and is the band's bass player, he got his nickname from another dangerous hobby he enjoys—blowing stuff up. His real name is Brick Ferdinand, with short curly hair and a stocky, refrigerator-like build typical of bass players. He earned his nickname last year when he was preparing some black powder and it went off sooner than expected. Nobody was hurt, but the government nearly deported him back to Canada. And no one will ever call him Brick again.

Iggy is Mark Fleece, a tall nerd with a wry smile and straight blond hair that's balding. He got his nickname because the band likes to play an Iggy Pop song in which Mark gleefully shouts out "Iggy" quite a few times. One day, a man stopped Mark on the streets of Palo Alto and said, "I know you." Mark thought the man was referring to some technical work, and he had no interest in pursuing such nerdiness with a stranger. He was planning to blow the guy off when the man brightened. "You're the guy who yells, 'Iggy.'" Now that was a different story. This was no nerdy stranger, he was a fan of the lab band, and the band doesn't get many fans. So Mark smirked and told him, "I *am* Iggy." We've been calling him that ever since.

* * *

One day at lunch, Red-Ink Vlad tells us he wants to ride his bike clear across the United States, from Silicon Valley to New York City. This isn't going to be a single trip, because that would be entirely too much time on a bike. Instead, he'll ride part way, then leave his bike somewhere and fly home. When he feels like riding some more, he'll fly back and ride farther east, eventually crossing the country.

The younger bikers in the lab take this as a challenge, and all of them decide to cross the country too. But rather than do it in easy pieces, they want to tear across the continent in five gut-rattling days of hard riding. Big Andy and Give Me All What We Have can't wait to depart. Iggy and Boom join as well, desirous of some American asphalt instead of their Canadian roads.

The idea circulates for days, each lunchtime discussion evoking bigger goals and louder brags until it's no longer a plan to cross the continent. It's now a race. Everyone will leave California at the same time, and the first to get to New York City wins. What they win is the dubious distinction of having won the race. Trophies and other prizes are not a factor.

Now Red-Ink Vlad, who suggested the idea of a cross-country trip, is less excited by a race. He's in his fifties and no longer finds that sort of competition necessary. But the other four are already dreaming of hog glory, and each time they tell him he doesn't need to enter the competition, it only makes him more determined to show up these young whippersnappers. Soon enough, he's in, too.

The race starts a week later. Five loud bikes sit in the lab parking lot, their side bags bulging and their riders fully geared. They shake hands all around, then they strap on helmets and depart. The rest of us hope to see our colleagues soon, and we try not to think about any trouble ahead.

In order to help the rest of the lab follow the race, each rider has a digital camera and one of these new global satellite phones that they've rigged to send pictures. They plan to stop at state crossings and send shots of themselves next to the welcome sign. That way, we can tell who is where. A few side-bets are being made around the lab, with Big Andy and Boom in the lead followed by Give Me All What We Have and Iggy. The odds have Red-Ink Vlad in last place; so just to be ornery, I put my money on him, which cheers him considerably.

The first progress reports come at the Nevada border where Big Andy leads the pack, as expected. The next three post similar photos soon after, but Red-Ink Vlad does not check in. They race down Interstate 80 and end the day sending pictures at the Utah border where they stop for the night. Vlad remains silent.

The next day, we get reports from the four leaders who enter Wyoming and power across the empty state toward the even emptier Nebraska. Everyone is starting to get concerned about Vlad, but suddenly he sends a picture of himself at the Nebraska state line, ahead of the others. Nobody said he had to check in at each crossing, so he's clearly been concentrating on racing, not on posting pictures. Still, there he is, smiling in his leathers with a giant "Welcome to Nebraska" behind him, the same sign that the other four send hours later when they report in. The race is getting interesting.

On the third day, the four younger men make it to Iowa and feel happy with their progress. Vlad is once again silent, but now I'm not worried as much. The fourth day takes them past Illinois and Indiana, leaving them in Ohio. One more day and the race will be over.

On the morning of the fifth day of the race, Vlad sends another picture. He's way out front, already in Pennsylvania, and I wonder if he's been bothering to sleep. The others enter the state a few hours later, but Vlad has a solid lead, and when night falls, he sends a picture of himself standing in New York's Times Square. Boom arrives three hours later to claim second place, minutes ahead of Big Andy who takes third. Give Me All What We Have is in fourth place, and Iggy brings up the rear. They spend the evening getting drunk, then they fly home the next day, their bikes loaded on a truck to save them the return trip.

The lab welcomes the five of them, and after a suitable amount of celebration, returns to work. Even the racers have had enough and are glad to sit at a computer for a while.

I'm discussing a technical issue with Red-Ink Vlad the following week, when I finally get around to talking about bikes. I want to know how he won the race, but I start easy and ask what he loves about riding.

He shrugs. "I like to ride so I can think." I suppose I already knew this because many of us in the lab have received phone calls from Vlad when he's out on the road, the rush of air suddenly uncovering something vital. A good number of the lab's papers have emerged from Vlad's calls at roadside phone booths, after which he hops back on the bike to resume his motorized meditation.

With the small talk dispatched, I get to the point and ask how he managed to beat the other four. He pauses, then he asks me to close the door.

"You were the only one who bet on me, so I owe you this. You know that I own four bikes. What you don't know is that I've always kept them around the country, in storage lockers or friends' garages. When I want to ride, I choose one of the bikes, take a plane to it, and ride it somewhere. Doesn't matter where. When I've had enough, I leave the bike with someone else, and I fly home. I've crossed the country numerous times but never straight through. I usually meander once I hit the road, and I often backtrack."

"So, what are you saying?" I'm trying to puzzle out his victory. "Years of experience have enabled you to ride the highways all night long? Is that how you won the race?"

Red-Ink Vlad lets out a single laugh. "No but having bikes all over the country let me win. I started the race by riding to the airport and flying to Cheyenne, Wyoming where one of my bikes sits in a friend's garage. I took it to the Nebraska border for a photo, then turned around and went to Colorado to leave the bike with another friend. Next, I flew to Cleveland where a second bike was waiting, the same model as the one I had at the start of the race, and that's the one I rode to New York City."

Bobblehead

I'm sitting at a hotel bar, wondering how long I can nurse my beer before the bartender's barely disguised look of exasperation pushes me to order another. It's a bad night for him since everyone in the bar is a light drinker, thanks to the tech conference that's mobbing the hotel and local restaurants. A crush of geeky men is buzzing around with a smattering of geeky women, letting loose in uninhibited ways they save for events of this magnitude. But even when they shed the workday jeans and T-shirts for the nerd-formal conference wear of slacks and button-down shirts, few of them are doing much drinking. In this crowd, a joint will get more attention than a round of drinks.

I'm near the bottom of the glass, and the crowd is starting to thin, when who should walk in but my coworker, N Hudson, strutting his lanky build like a newly crowned king. His first name starts with N, but he's never told any of us what it stands for, so we're left calling him N, which works all around. He's got a boyish face and normal-length brown hair that's noticeable in this gathering of long-haired nerds. At work, he likes to dress up a bit more than average, with sweater vests and proper leather shoes, so his conference wear is positively excessive, with a ruffled shirt and a bow tie. Heads turn briefly when he enters the bar, but in the fashion-vacuum of a tech gathering, nobody trusts their own opinion, so they take a requisite glance then turn away.

N scans the bar with his back arched and head pointed so far up that I wonder if he's about to fall over. When he notices me, he stands straight for the first time, then races to the seat next to mine faster than a slingshot-launched water balloon.

Now I am not an unfriendly person, especially when I've made it nearly through a pint of beer, so I open up the conversation. "You're looking fully charged, N. What's the word?"

"The word? Gee!" He always speaks quickly, but tonight, he's running hot. "There's so much more going on than just a word, but if you need it boiled down to something that atomic, then the word is mega!" His palpable energy, along with his use of a tech prefix applied by nerds to achieve a vague sense of scale where none exists, tells me that he's got plenty to say but has no idea how to express it. I mean, look at him! He's so excited that spittle is gathering at the corners of his mouth, forcing me to lean away in the vain hope that a few more inches of distance will protect me from his enthusiastic slobber.

At this point in the conversation, I could ask him about his word choice. Instead I take another sip of beer as a way of indicating that if he doesn't explain more, and fast, I'll have to order a second drink to continue my self-medication. N turns to the bartender and soon has a glass of something dark and bubbly which, knowing him, means an undoctored cola. He'll go all night on that, growing even more animated as the sugar rush deepens. I, unfortunately, will be glazed and unresponsive if this story takes long.

N sips his sweet fizz then rolls on. "Mega. A single word that says so much. This conference is the place to be, for sure. I almost didn't get to come this year because of budget cutbacks. Management made a rule that only authors presenting papers could attend. But I worked my magic and look!" He spreads his arms as evidence.

His explanation helps somewhat, but I rarely see people this jazzed to be at a tech conference. In any case, he's talking, so I wait for more. But N is elsewhere as he savors his drink, so I let him load up, hoping that he'll explain why he's this excited.

N doesn't disappoint. "You know who else is here? Alil! We both decided to submit papers and make this into a vacation. That's why this conference is so great. We've been looking forward to some time together, away from work. Alil has it all planned, our own personal party."

"So where is she?" I'm scanning the bar, but she's nowhere to be seen. Her real name is Lila Judd, and she chose the nickname Alil by reversing the letters of Lila. She's a reasonable person with the good sense to avoid too much nerd jargon. Her straight brown hair falls like a curtain around her shoulders, and she rarely dresses in anything but a T-shirt and jeans, the sort of look that everyone sports these days, so I give her full credit.

N waves his hand to discourage my search for Alil. "Her talk is tomorrow morning, so she went to sleep early. Big day and all." He rocks from side to side like a rare animal performing an obscure mating dance.

There's only one problem with N's story. His paper got rejected, which means he really did have to work some kind of magic to be here. I could mention this and ask how he arranged the trip without being an author, but I'm more interested in him and Alil, who I've thought might make a good couple. She and N have been working together on a project, and the way they tease each other makes everyone in the lab figure they're already connected, but you never know when it comes to nerds.

Curious to learn more, I lean forward into the spittle zone. "You two finally an item?"

"Ach." He slaps the bar to dispel any unverified rumors. "We're just friends. But *good* friends." His emphasis suggests their relationship teeters on the edge of the friend zone and could fall squarely onto the more-than-friend side with the slightest gust of wind. I briefly wonder whether Alil would agree with this assessment, but according to N, she setup some sort of arrangement here, so there might actually be consent.

I brave another inch toward the white foam, now so thick in the corners of his mouth it's threatening to dribble down his chin. "And?" I keep my question simple to clear space for N's elaboration.

He sets down his glass. "Check this out. Five years old and more of a collector's item than ever." Reaching into his oversize messenger bag, he pulls out a Yoda bobblehead, still in its original packaging which is frayed but holding together. "I scored this little gem when the movie came out. Probably the rarest piece in my collection."

I'm aware of N's interest in bobbleheads. He's got a dozen of them decorating his desk at work, and he boasts of many more at home. His passion, his grail, is the unopened package. I can tell this one's rare.

I pick up the box to give it a little shake so the spring-loaded head with cartoon-scale ears can knock around in its extra wide packaging. I'm beginning to see where this story is going. "So you're giving this to Alil?"

N reels back and stares at me like I've grown two extra heads and a second asshole. "Are you kidding? Alil isn't into bobbleheads! She likes snow globes!" He spits out this information as if it's such common knowledge that I must be beyond clueless to be so ignorant. I'm willing to admit

I'm wrong about Alil, but in that case, I still don't see how the bobblehead figures in his convoluted story.

N seeks relief from his glass of treacly water. To show my solidarity, I finish my beer. When the empty glass lands safely on the table, I continue the inquiry. "OK, then. Let's see the snow globe." I peer into his messenger bag, wondering whether this conversation is going somewhere or is just a random collection of unrelated details.

N quickly stashes the bobblehead and shakes his head as he closes the bag. "I don't collect snow globes, and Alil's got a huge number of them. I doubt I could get one she doesn't already have." He chugs the rest of his soda and gets up to leave. "Well, see you tomorrow."

Wait! That's it? Perhaps this *is* a random collection of unrelated details. I'm beginning to wonder if there's more than one beer in my bloodstream. Did I miss something, or is N failing to make any sense? Before I can determine the answer, N has wandered out of the bar, still strutting like he owns the place. I try to puzzle it out, but in the end, I escape to my room.

Soon after returning from the conference, it becomes common knowledge in the lab that N and Alil are indeed an item. I feel happy for them, and I don't give the relationship another thought. But a few days later, I'm on my way down the hall when I spy something very familiar sitting on a desk. So familiar that I'm forced to back up and take a better look. There it is, the Yoda bobblehead, still in the frayed packaging. And this isn't N's office, it's Mild Verduin's, a man so incredibly bland that everyone calls him Mild instead of his real name, Miles. He always wears the same gray pants and shirt over his portly body, although those who have been brave enough to visit his dwelling have reported that he has an entire closet of gray pants and gray shirts, so at least he's clean.

Mild was also at the conference, but I couldn't bring myself to see his talk because he speaks so slowly that I would have certainly fallen asleep. Right now, however, my curiosity overcomes my desire to remain awake, so I step inside. We chat for a while about tech, then I nod toward the new addition on his desk.

"So, you collect bobbleheads?"

"I'm just getting started." His slow, measured words are already making me drowsy. "But this one ..." He pats the box lovingly. "A true collector's item. Got it from N."

"I see. And why did N give this to you? Looks rare and expensive."

"Definitely." He smiles. "Got it for typing N's name. Hardly any keystrokes at all." He lifts both hands from the keyboard and raises his fingers one-by-one as he recites the letters. "N. H-U-D-S-O-N. Just seven letters and I've got this awesome bobblehead. Know what I mean?"

I do not, and I give him my best sideways look, hands on my hips, silently waiting for more of an explanation. But Mild has fewer social skills than his Yoda doll, so I'm forced to ask him directly.

"OK, I'll bite. How did typing his name earn you this bobblehead?"

"You don't know?" He chortles like a demented scientist, which he may well be now that I think about it, especially if he convinced N to give him a rare bobblehead for seven taps of a keyboard.

He wiggles in his seat then leans closer. "In exchange for getting this delightful little object, I wrote N's name at the top of my conference paper, right under my own name. That made him my second author."

Proper Ron

I'm sitting in the living room of a new Sunnyvale home, recently bought by Pizza Man and his wife Franny. He and I were graduate students in Pittsburgh a few years ago, but now all of us have migrated to Silicon Valley where the winters are far less harsh and the summer heat is dry and tolerable. His real name is Manuel Cucinotta, a stocky bearded man with black curly hair and a wicked grin he likes to flash, especially when he has his arm around the taller, thinner, and long-brunette-tressed Franny. Since he helped pay for school by working at the campus pizzeria, he got dubbed Pizza Manuel and soon after, just Pizza Man. He may have a high-paying tech job now, but he'll always be Pizza Man, and to prove it, he's making one tonight.

As our host and cook, he's in and out of the living room while he prepares dinner. At one point when he's in the kitchen, Franny and I hear him cursing like a crazed pirate. We get up to look, but as soon as we enter the kitchen, we laugh. There's a big sloppy splat of pizza dough half draped over the stove, stretching down the edge like one of Dali's melting clocks.

Pizza Man tries to peel it off. "I can't believe it! I haven't done this in years."

Franny smirks. "I told you your pizza twirling skills were getting rusty."

He flaps his hands in a brief sign of helplessness, then he finishes scraping off what he can and returns the dough to the pan. "This is definitely going to be a Proper Ron pizza."

Proper Ron? There's someone I haven't heard from since my school days. Portly and balding, Ron speaks softly in a refined, almost Patrician way, so completely proper that we made it part of his name. Yet, for all his propriety, he's the nicest nerd I've ever met. When he finished school, he stayed in Pittsburgh for work, because he had to. While most of us naturally gravitated to Silicon Valley, Ronald Scaife III is firmly anchored in Pittsburgh, a descendant of a long-established family. He even jokes about Carnegie-Mellon's Mudge Hall where many of the graduate students are housed. To him, it's his aunt's house where he played as a child before Uncle Ed and Aunt Pauline Mudge moved away and donated the building to the university. Proper Ron doesn't think of the Mudges, the Scaifes, the Mellons, and even the Carnegies as the uber-rich of Pittsburgh. They're just family.

So I have to ask why the scion of Pittsburgh's old money has a pizza pie named after him. A messy, failed pizza pie. It seems like an insult.

Pizza Man doesn't answer immediately but spends a little time rearranging the dough so it covers the pan. Keeping his mouth tight, he applies tomato sauce, cheese, and various toppings. When he's finally got the pie in the oven, he grabs his glass of wine to take a relaxing sip, then we return to the living room.

"You know," he explains. "I grew up poor and had to work extra jobs during graduate school."

I nod at him. "I always appreciated your other job as the department pot dealer."

"Yeah, I managed just fine. But I was truly bowled over the night Proper Ron threw a party at his penthouse apartment."

Proper Ron's place was indeed notable. I, and all of the other students, were living modestly in small dormitory rooms, shared off-campus rentals, or if we were lucky, private rooms. But not Proper Ron. He lived in an elegant high-rise apartment building with a doorman, private parking, and stellar views of the city from a penthouse balcony. We might have teased someone else about being able to afford such a place, but not Ron. First of all, although he did come from spectacular amounts of money, he often pointed out that by the time it had filtered through the generations, it wasn't as grand as it once was. And he lived stylishly because his parents refused to allow anything less. But the real reason we love and respect Proper Ron is that, beyond being a very sharp thinker, he's also terribly sweet—a computing saint—gracious, generous, and never lording over anyone.

One day I asked Proper Ron if he had any others in his family and was surprised to find out he's an only child. When I asked why, Ron sheepishly shrugged. "My father always said, 'Tried it once, didn't like it.'" How can we tease someone who makes jokes like that about himself?

Pizza Man continues his story. "I'm at Proper Ron's party, dazzled by the view from up there, and I'm thinking he has everything he could ever want. But I'm wrong. He takes me aside and tells me that he's always wanted to learn how to twirl pizza dough so he could make his own pies."

Franny chuckles. "There's no need to twirl pizza dough. You can roll it out and spread it on the pan much more easily. Of course, the pizza pros, including this guy,"—she elbows her husband—"like to twirl it, but it's mostly for show."

"Hey, give me some credit!" Pizza Man smiles at her, clearly a repartee they've done before. "Twirling airs the dough better, which makes it taste more authentic. Also, twirling helps make it round. If you roll it out, you're going to have more ragged edges, but if you twirl it, it lays perfectly in the pan." He kisses his fingers then flicks his hand outward in a gesture reminiscent of fancy chefs everywhere.

"So you agreed to teach Proper Ron how to twirl, but he sucked at it so badly that you now invoke his name for your failed pies?"

"Actually, I refused to teach him. First of all, it's not a skill you can easily pick up. You ruin a lot of dough before you can make a perfect pie. Second, the owner of the shop made me pay for every failed twirl. He loved the fact that I could do it because it made his shop more authentic. But each time I couldn't catch it properly, he'd dock my pay. So there was no way I was going to let Proper Ron ruin a small fortune in pizza dough."

I'm confused by any sentence that combines saving money while mentioning the most financially comfortable student at the school. "Proper Ron could afford it. Why didn't you tell the boss you'd pay double for every ruined ball of dough?"

"Well," Pizza Man sighs. "The real problem was the boss wouldn't let me giving lessons to anyone. He enjoyed having a unique niche among pizza shops because of me. If I trained someone else, it would cut into his business. So he warned me that he'd fire me if I tried to teach twirling."

"OK, so Proper Ron taught himself, right? And naturally, he sucks at it."

Pizza Man and Franny laugh together, then she nods at me. "Manuel *did* teach Proper Ron to twirl."

"Sad but true." Pizza Man downs the last of his wine and ducks into the kitchen to peek at the baking pie. He returns with a full glass and raises it to us. "To Proper Ron. The only person I ever taught to twirl pizza dough."

"Really?" I sip my wine, waiting to find out how.

"Yeah, really. I came into work one day a few months later, and Proper Ron was in one of the shop's red-and-white aprons. The boss introduced us as if we'd never met, then told me that Ron was new and needed to be taught. Totally blew me away."

"Aha! That makes sense. He went for on-the-job training. But I'm guessing he still sucked at it."

Pizza Man slaps his forehead. "The worst. I watched him toss about three hundred pies over the next few days before he gave up and quit. Only one of them survived long enough to become a pizza. Proper Ron could roll it out and even give it a nice toss, but they all landed badly. Poor guy couldn't catch the dough, no pun intended."

"Seriously? Hundreds of wasted dough balls?" I tilt my head. "How did Proper Ron manage to stay on the job that long without getting fired? Did he pay double for the wasted flips?"

"No, he didn't have to pay anything for the dough."

"Yes he did!" Franny levels a stare at Pizza Man and wags a finger. "He'd bought the pizza shop, which made him the boss—he paid dearly for that dough."

The Two-Headed Nerd

I'm the last one in the lunch room, ready to finish up and leave when John rushes in and settles down to eat. Naturally, I stay to talk since it shows poor manners to walk away after someone has worked this hard to make it to the table. John is a recent hire from Caltech and has gotten this nickname because the computer science students there are amused by the movie, *Buckaroo Banzai*, where aliens try to fit into human society by naming each of themselves John. In honor of this joke, the Caltech students have rewritten their door tags, so their first name is now John. As you walk down the halls past the student offices, you see John Detmore, John Amos, John Guggenheim, John Sutter, and plenty more. And even though the person eating lunch with me, John Guggenheim, has graduated and now works in our lab, a good nickname is impossible to shake, particularly in this situation because John's real name is Victoria Guggenheim, and yes, John is a woman.

John is tall, with blonde hair that cups her face, and she stares at you with intensity when she speaks, leaving people impressed with both her delivery and her content. Today, however, she seems flustered, so I wait a bit to let those first few bites take the edge off whatever is bothering her. Just as I'm about to make some light conversation to shatter the silence, she charges forward.

"Can you explain something to me?" Her voice rings with a mild level of annoyance. "What's the deal with Doiley Carte?"

Aha, now this is a good question. John wants to understand the two-headed nerd in our lab who we have affectionately named Doiley Carte. Simply put, a two-headed nerd is a pair of scientists who work well together. There are two-headed nerds all over the computing landscape these days, for example Bill Gates and Paul Allen or Steve Jobs and Steve Wozniak. And outside of computing, there are plenty of duos such as the Curies, or Crick and Watson. Even Edison and Tesla were a team, but of course, they hated each other.

When it comes to a two-headed nerd, you can't hire one of them, you have to hire both. They work together, think together, and publish together, coauthoring many papers. In our lab, the two-headed nerd is the powerhouse team of Michael Doiley and Roger Carte, or as we like to call them, Doiley Carte. Any reference to the Gilbert and Sullivan troupe with the same name but slightly different spelling is purely intentional, especially since Roger Carte has a side hobby of singing in an amateur theater group and chants Gilbert and Sullivan songs with a goofy grin whenever the opportunity arises. A few months ago, his musical outbursts would be accompanied by Michael Doiley, the two thin and bespectacled nerds stumbling around the floor in an awkward attempt to dance, the taller and bearded Carte barely moving as the clean-shaven Doiley zips about. Lately, however, they've been keeping their distance, and nobody knows why. They still pump out brilliant papers, but they can often be heard arguing behind closed doors.

Regardless of how Michael Doiley and Roger Carte feel about each other, everyone in the lab loves them, and we mean no disrespect when we call them Doiley Carte. We're merely dropping the word "and," which nerds love to do in an effort to pack as much information as possible into every waking moment.

Since John is new in the lab and working directly with Roger Carte, I can understand why she wants to learn more about these two, so I start easy.

"In my experience, two-headed nerds generally have the same pattern, and Doiley Carte is no exception. One head has the brains, and the other head has the mouth. You've been hired to work with Roger Carte, the brains of the operation. He's soft-spoken, kind, and always polite, which is why we call him Mr. Rogers. And he's an absolute genius, which also elevates him in our opinion."

John nods. "Yeah, I get that part, and I'm really enjoying working with Mr. Rogers. But I haven't spent enough time with Michael Doiley to know the deal. He never stops talking, and half the stuff he says makes him seem like an absolute idiot."

I laugh. "That's why we call him Doublespeed Doiley. He's one of those guys who has no technological filters, and probably no filters about anything, for that matter. He says whatever is on his mind, so you're right when you say half the ideas he suggests are bull-droppings. But every once in a while, he delivers a gem, and when he does, Mr. Rogers is smart enough to grab it and run."

"Oh, please!" John's about to take another bite of lunch but pauses, the sandwich hovering in the air. "Mr. Rogers is able to think on his own. I've seen him sit in a meeting and say nothing until the conversation has dwindled to near silence, then he offers a timid pronouncement that explains everything perfectly. The guy is beyond genius, and I can't believe he isn't the originator of most of their work." She brightens and raises her finger. "What about that stuff he did with audio transforms? I'm sure it was his idea."

I shake my head slowly, hating to disappoint. "That was Doublespeed Doiley. He was making his usual irrelevant noise one day when he suddenly gazed into space and said he wondered if different audio transforms could be combined successfully. Mr. Rogers practically beamed with heavenly light, and he's been working on it ever since."

John slams her fist against the table. "Damn it! Are you saying Mr. Rogers has never had an original idea?"

I shrug. "He's never had the chance. Doublespeed Doiley's always around spouting thoughts first."

She hesitates before going on. "This makes me worry that I'm breaking up an important team. I'm just starting my career, so I don't want to be the one who upset the Doiley Carte."

"Cute." I snicker at her joke. "But whatever happens to them is not your fault. Those two were totally enthusiastic about hiring you, both at the start of the search process when they were insistent that Mr. Rogers needed someone else to work with, and at the end when they'd found you and decided to make an offer. It was a total no-brainer because both were impressed with your chops."

"Well, I guess I fooled them because now that I'm here, I'm ruining everything."

I simply don't believe this to be true. "You're wrong, John. You've been doing your job, and that's what you should keep doing. Stay away from the interpersonal Doiley Carte relationship and focus on the research. It may be awkward working with half of an established team, but this is what they wanted. If you can emerge from this as someone who gets work done, you win."

John seems to ponder my advice as she finishes lunch. I wish her well dealing with our two-headed nerd, then I return to my office.

A few weeks later, I see an internal tech report go by, a work in progress that's not ready for publication. Most good ideas start this way, and many such reports get issued on a nearly daily basis, but this one is unusual because of an unexpected set of authors: Roger Carte and Victoria Guggenheim. It's the first time Mr. Rogers has written anything without Doublespeed Doiley as his coauthor, and it's every bit as good as a Doiley Carte effort. I run into John in the hall soon after and congratulate her on the work.

"Thanks." She looks around nervously, then waves me into her office. When we're out of sight, she throws her head into her hands to cover gathering tears. After a long sigh, she groans, "It's all falling apart."

"Come on! Your paper was excellent. You still think you're ruining the magic of Doiley Carte?"

"I know it. Mr. Rogers may be a genius, but he gets depressed, and he's snippy with Doublespeed Doiley. I noticed he printed his resume the other day, so I'm worried he's going to quit. Meanwhile, Doublespeed Doiley hates me and won't talk about anything technical. Last week at lunch, he was rambling about numerical analysis, but as soon as I walked in, he changed the subject to a movie he'd seen. I'm telling you the guy hates me."

This is indeed fishy, as Doublespeed Doiley never avoids a technical discussion, even with toddlers and animals. I saw him explain gravity to a rock once, but it remained unmoved. And if Mr. Rogers is leaving the lab, that would be a hard loss. But I still don't see this as John's fault.

"Look, you were hired to work with Mr. Rogers, so Doublespeed Doiley's feelings are not your problem. Whatever is going on between them is their story, not yours. Don't worry."

"Don't worry! That's easy for you to say, you're not getting fired. They barely tolerate me here." Her mouth scrunches. "Should I put the work with Mr. Rogers on my resume, or should I leave it off so people don't think I'm a trouble maker?"

Oh, great. She's cleaning up her resume and getting ready to quit. The lab is still forming; we can't afford to lose people faster than we hire them. I need to make her see that the situation is not so dire.

"OK, calm down. They're not going to fire you, especially if Mr. Rogers quits, because you're the one who's been collaborating with him. People will want your insight on the work he left behind. Personally, I think it's great that you're rearranging the Doiley Carte playing field, but rest assured, your job is not in danger."

She sniffs. "That's not what Doublespeed Doiley said."

"Oh, what did he say besides a movie review?"

"He cornered me in the hallway and went all cowboy, saying this lab isn't big enough for the three of us. I'm sure he knows Mr. Rogers is upset and thinking of quitting, so he probably figures if I quit first, life can get back to normal. It's true; I have to go. I may not be at fault, but people won't see it that way when they hear that I was the factor that broke up Doiley and Carte."

"Come on, John ..." I'm suddenly struck by the absurdity of her nickname so I start again. "Sorry, *Victoria*. It will also look bad if you go job-hunting only a few months after starting work here. Employers will want to know why. Better to stay where you are and let the pieces fall where they may. People are pretty impressed with this first paper by Carte and Guggenheim. Stick to the science and you'll be fine."

John agrees that my point is valid, but this toxic environment isn't what she signed up for, so it's time to go. She already has a job interview at SunTex tomorrow, so her work here may soon be ending. I wish her well.

The next day, I pass Mr. Rogers's office as he steps out with a fat envelope in his hands. He cheerfully tells me that he's collected some of his best work, then he leaves the building. That looks to me like a man seeking work, so I have to admit John may be right. Mr. Rogers is leaving us, which makes me sad.

Three days later, as I'm wandering past John's office, she waves me in energetically, an excited look on her face.

I get comfortable in the chair across from her desk. "Did you get the job?"

John laughs. "Yes and no. I got the job, but I'm not taking it. You'll never guess who I saw there! I'm walking around the SunTex offices, checking the place out, and there he was, also interviewing."

I know, of course, because I saw Mr. Rogers leaving with his best work in hand. John was right in predicting the end of the Doiley Carte. This has probably been the first time Mr. Rogers has looked for work on his own, without his famed mouthpiece.

I tell this to John, but she chuckles at my supposition. "No, you've got it backward. Mr. Rogers isn't looking for work; it's Doublespeed Doiley who's leaving. That's what he meant when he said this lab wasn't big enough for the three of us. It wasn't a threat, it was a concession. He's been planning on quitting for some time now and only stayed until Mr. Rogers and I could get comfortable working together."

"But what about Mr. Rogers' resume? I saw him heading out with a big pile of work."

"Yeah, he did get that job. He was applying to be director of his little theater group. The work he had was his favorite musical arrangements. But he's not leaving the lab."

"It's funny," John continues. "When Doublespeed Doiley saw me interviewing there, he pulled me aside and explained everything. The friction they've had is all because Mr. Rogers wants to come up with his own ideas, and that can't happen with the two of them working together. Doublespeed Doiley tried to keep his mouth shut, but it just didn't work."

I laugh. "His brain never stops churning, and his mouth hasn't got a disconnect switch."

John smiles. "Yep, it was impossible. So Mr. Rogers demanded to work with someone else, and they hired me. He further demanded, before I arrived, that Doublespeed Doiley avoid technical talk with me because he was trying to mute the flow of ideas. That explains why he seemed so rude all the time.

"Doublespeed Doiley assured me he was never angry, and he apologized if I'd gotten the wrong idea. But his relationship with Mr. Rogers was already damaged, so he knew he needed to leave. He's looking forward to working with a new group of people he can motivate with his steady stream of babble. He practically begged me to keep my job here because, he said, Mr. Rogers would be crushed if I quit. Then he congratulated me on our recent tech report and predicted the two of us would be the next two-headed nerd. It really cheered me up."

Game Night

Alil bounces into my office, her long brown hair twirling wildly. With an ear-to-ear smile, she swings an arm over the top of her head and slaps a party invitation on my desk. "It's game night at our group house." Then she springs out the door.

I'm not much of a game player, but Alil and her housemates live in the foothills where they plan to play board games like Monopoly and Risk, card games like poker, and conceptual games like Diplomacy or Dungeons and Dragons. I'll make an appearance, but I doubt I'll stay long.

On the night of the party, the nerd house is decorated excessively. Little signs direct us to the proper places to play, eat, and smoke (outdoors, please). Within each room, the games pieces are setup precisely. Even the snack dishes, heavily scented of sugar and spice, are labeled abundantly with names, ingredients, and recommended game pairings. This party can run itself, which is what the hosts want, because they plan to play all night and don't want to have to explain rules to newbies.

I walk into the card room as Alil is chatting with Blue, a researcher whose primary focus is on women in computing. Blue is actually Susan Andoria, but since her last name evokes a *Star Trek* alien that's blue, the nerds can't help but call her that. It doesn't matter that her short blonde hair and her dark outfits are never that color; she's Blue.

Alil notices me and sheepishly gestures around the room. "Sorry we weren't able to create a full Vegas experience." I'm not sure what part of Vegas she thinks this isn't, because I see every piece of gambling paraphernalia: chips and a chip rake, a croupier's vest and visor, a dimly lit green baize table, and a card shoe that can hold hundreds of cards. There's even a well-stocked bar along the side of the room.

I laugh. "If this isn't the full Vegas experience, then what's missing besides cocktail waitresses, security grunts, and stage shows?"

Alil smirks. "It's the financial scale that's non-Vegas. You can't lose too much playing penny-ante poker. In a typical night, you'll lose no more than five dollars, although someone once lost twenty because they got reckless. But people win, too, so have a seat."

I understood the small-time aspect of this game before coming tonight. The Mountain, who's played cards with Alil, explained the rules. He even told me something that I found unbelievable, so I ask to be sure. "Is it true that everyone cheats at cards here?"

"Well ..." She rubs her chin. "I don't know if I'd call it cheating. Most of us have learned to count cards, so we have an advantage."

Blue snaps her head to look at Alil. "Counting cards? Are you saying you can remember every card in the deck?"

Alil laughs. "No, card counting is much simpler than that. Sure, some people could probably memorize a whole deck, but most of us just do a simplified version where the low-value cards—two through five—get a negative bump, the middle-value cards—six through nine—get no bump, and the high-value cards—ten and up—get a positive bump. You start at zero, then for each card you see, either add one, subtract one, or do nothing. It's easy. If the number gets too high or too low, you know that the other kind of card is more likely to appear."

Blue stares with wide eyes, so Alil summarizes the lesson. "It's not cheating, it's probability and statistics."

I shake my head as I point out one missing detail. "You know, if you count cards like that in Vegas, they'll break your kneecaps. So I'd say it's cheating."

"Oh." Alil fidgets a bit and sips her cola.

Blue reaches for the card shoe. "What's this?"

"A card shoe helps you deal quickly, see?" Alil deals a few cards to demonstrate, then she opens the cover to show that it's got six decks of cards awaiting play. Caught by some activity in another room, she wanders off while Blue plays with the shoe, dealing out cards and pretending she's running a game. She even mutters gambling lingo in a failed attempt to sound professional.

I soon leave the room. The last thing I need is to be taken by a bunch of mathematically inclined nerds who don't think they're cheating. And it's good I get out when I can, because ten minutes later, Alil announces the card room to everyone, and all the wannabe poker-stars head in.

I wander around and indulge in a game of Yahtzee, then I sit and watch as a game of Monopoly wraps up. Games may not be my specialty, but at least the food and drinks are good, and everyone's having fun.

An hour later, I wander back to the card room to find Blue sitting alone, counting a big pile of cash. Contrary to the this-is-not-Vegas sentiment, she's got a thick stack of twenty-dollar bills.

"Did you win all that?" I sit down next to her and admire the haul.

"Yep, took them for over fifty dollars each." She waves a fan of cash in the air.

"But I though everyone was cheating. Did you cheat, too?"

"Of course, but I didn't count cards. I counted something else."

I tilt my head. "What would that be?"

"I counted on the fact that everyone *else* was counting cards." Blue offers a modest smile. "I rearranged the cards in the shoe so the card counters would have an incorrect sense of the deck. Then I notched a card just past that section and arranged the remaining cards in a pattern only I knew. During play, I bluffed a few times and lost to make everyone distrust my big bets. Then, when the notched card got dealt, I knew exactly what would come next and what everyone else would think was coming. That was my opportunity to bet the moon and take them all."

Plagiarism

Nobody likes Earache, which is why the nerds gave him that nickname. He's loud, he's annoying, and most of the time, he's so full of bull that it leaves everyone snickering behind his back. He can enter a room, all proud of himself, and blurt out a pronouncement heavy with tech words and acronyms, then give us a smug look that assures everyone of his brilliance. But when I roll his words back in my mind, I find nothing but nonsense, each word standing tall on its own but struggling with the others to form a cohesive thought. It never works.

Earache's real name is Eric Deerfield. He's an average-size man with a Fu Manchu mustache and thin, receding hair that's poorly groomed, giving him a crazy-old-guy look. To make matters worse, he dresses more formally than most, in button-downs instead of the usual T-shirts, but he wears these outfits sloppily, his shirt never more than half-tucked into his pants, his pants dating back to a time when he was shorter and his feet didn't extend as far beyond the cuffs.

Nobody can figure out how Earache's been this successful, with a doctorate and a position of respect in the lab. Some are baffled that he managed to earn any degree, but those who've also matriculated from the education mill know that perseverance can make up for intelligence, demonstrating that even the highest of academic degrees is meaningless. There's an old joke that the BS degree is *bullshit*, the MS is *more shit*, and the PhD is *piled higher and deeper*. But beyond validating the joke, the more common bewilderment among folks in the lab is how Earache managed to get a job *here*. My only conclusion is he leveraged the degree to get in the door, then somehow seemed wise even though he's got the intelligence of a sock.

Regardless of how it happened, Earache works here, so everyone is forced to take extreme measures to keep him at a safe distance. N is only two offices away from Earache, with an unoccupied space in between because nobody wants to share a common wall with that loudmouth. N sits far enough away that the sound doesn't bother him, but when Earache's feeling lonely and nobody's come to hear his pseudo-brilliant ideas, he roams the hall, and his first victim is always N.

One day while Earache is camped in N's office delivering mindless chatter, N pretends to see something important on his screen and picks up his phone to dial Earache's office. When Earache hears his phone ring, he runs off to get it, and N happily returns to work. But the second time he does it, Earache figures it out, so N is forced to work harder. He knows the lab's main computer has a new telephone interface, so he writes a program to dial Earache's office phone. Now, he doesn't have to do anything suspicious, such as picking up his phone and having Earache's ring. There's nothing unusual about typing and clicking, and few know that computers can control phones at this point. N has created the world's first robocaller.

After that, whenever Earache shows up to pontificate, N discretely runs his program, forcing Earache to race back to his office for that all-important call. As usual, the phone stops ringing seconds before he can answer it, but at least he's safely back in his office where he will forget why he wandered the hall in the first place and will stay put for a while. Anyone else who might be in N's office at the time knows exactly what's going on, and they all share a laugh over the magical incantation that makes Earache disappear.

Today, however, a much more annoyed Earache stomps the hall. Instead of his usual disinformation, he's spouting anger. Loudly, of course. After he passes my office, I sneak out to the hall and watch from a safe distance as he gathers people in a meeting room to make his case. I don't need to go in there because I can hear him from where I stand. And even at this distance, he may have good cause for outrage.

"Someone stole my paper!" He's so incensed, I wonder if he's going to burst a blood vessel. "I did brilliant work, as always, and submitted it to this year's hardware conference. First, those nincompoops rejected the paper, giving me no reason at all. Then they *published it* but *took my name off it!* Look at this! Why is this Finnegan guy claiming to have written my paper?"

I scoot back to my office to find my copy of the conference proceedings. It's still sitting in my mail pile, so I tear open the package and start to read. Sure enough, the table of contents lists a paper by someone named James Finnegan. I'm curious to know why he stole Earache's work, so I flip to the first page where I immediately notice Professor James Finnegan is at Oceanview University in Oceanview, Kansas. I'm already laughing because this alleged Finnegan has delivered a slap in the face that Earache truly deserves.

I turn to the paper, wondering if it's any good. Given that Earache wrote it, I have my doubts. But someone published it, so perhaps there's something worthwhile. The paper starts off reasonably, with an abstract that makes more sense than Earache ever does. The introductory paragraphs are even sensible, with no evidence of the terminology eructation he usually delivers. I had no idea that Earache could think this clearly.

But as I read on, little tidbits start to emerge that reveal a different perspective. This paper is total blarney, written by someone with a finely tuned sense of humor. The author gathers the usual set of background information and assembles it in a more-or-less reasonable way. But soon enough, Professor Finnegan takes a left turn and drives off the road. By the end of the paper, the concluding sentence is so insane that I'm laughing out loud. This is a brilliant piece of bullsquatchi, far superior to anything I've ever heard Earache say. But he claims to have written every word, except the author's name and affiliation. This demands investigation.

I spend some time trying but failing to locate Professor Finnegan. There is no Oceanview University anywhere in the world, and I don't have to do any research to know there's no city of Oceanview in Kansas. I'm pointing this out at lunch a few days later when Endian starts to pay close attention even though he's at the other end of a long table and is in the middle of a different conversation.

Endian is Don Levi, an Israeli with a thick accent, black curly hair that's always a mess, and a beard shadow never less than three days old. His early work questioned how a number like 2134 would get sent between computers. The "big endian" method starts at the big end (the 2) and the "little endian" method starts at the 4. The word "endian" comes from *Gulliver's Travels* where the hero encounters an island of tiny people who argue about which end of an egg to crack when eating it. Don has borrowed the word, and it has become his nickname.

After lunch, Endian beckons me into his office. I haven't had many conversations with him, but I'm curious to learn more about this paper, so I follow him. He closes his door. "Do you know about the paper Earache submitted last year?"

Last year? I thought he was going to tell me about this year's workshop. I confess ignorance of such a paper, never having seen anything published by Earache in this conference or anywhere else.

"Aha." Endian smiles. "His paper last year was rejected because he had stolen mine."

"He did what?" I'm shocked that people do this, so I ask for clarification.

Endian rubs his chin. "Well, you know how it is in the printer room. You send something to be printed, then you get distracted and forget. It can be hours before you remember to go pick it up. That's why they have little cubbyholes, so unclaimed stuff doesn't end up in the trash. Anyway, last year I printed a version of my paper, forgot to get it, then made further changes and submitted it to the conference. I completely forgot about the copy I'd printed because it was already obsolete."

"You think Earache found that paper in the printer room and put his name on it?" This would be a pretty serious accusation.

"I know he did. Don't forget that I'm on the conference committee, so I get to see every paper that's submitted. Naturally, I can't review my own work, but I see loads of others, especially ones closest to my technical area. And one of the submissions I was given was that earlier version of my own paper, forgotten in the printer room, with Eric Deerfield listed as the author."

"Whoa! You must have been steamed."

Endian grumbles. "It was pretty shocking. I discussed it with the others on the committee, but not all of them accepted my version of the story. And since the committee was faced with two nearly identical papers by different authors, they decided to reject both. So yes, I was steamed."

I see where this is heading. "You're saying he stole your paper last year, so you stole his paper this year."

"Me steal *his* paper?" Endian laughs so hard that he begins coughing. When he's able to calm somewhat, he smiles. "I just wanted to get back at him for last year, that's all. I printed another paper and intentionally left it in the printer room. But this time, I sent a copy to the rest of the conference committee, so everyone would be on the lookout. Sure enough, Earache stole the paper again, put his name on it, and submitted it. And when his submission had the exact same words as the paper I'd given them, they finally believed my story. I'm happy to report that Eric Deerfield has been permanently banned from the conference."

"And what about you? You've worked on new stuff. Did you get a paper in this year?"

Endian waves the question away with a sneer. "I'm through with those people after they wouldn't listen to me last year, so I didn't submit to them. I guess I've been banned too, but the committee doesn't know that yet. I switched to a different conference."

I'm beginning to understand what happened. "Except you *did* get published, didn't you? I read a brilliant and devious paper, a work of great comic value that for some reason got past the review committee and made it into the proceedings."

Endian blushes. "I'm glad you liked it. That's the paper I wrote to bait Earache with subtle jokes and plenty of drivel.

I wanted the committee to notice it when they saw it again, so I tried to make it memorable. What I didn't expect was that they would be so amused they'd publish it anyway. They certainly couldn't put Earache's name on it, and I really didn't want mine there, so I made up Professor Finnegan and his ridiculous university. That way, everyone who starts to read it knows what to expect."

He leans back in his chair, smiling broadly. "It's turning out to be quite popular. I may have a future in tech comedy." Then he darkens and leans toward me. "But here's the strangest part of this whole affair. Earache retyped the entire paper from the pages I left in the printer room and not once did he realize it was a joke."

Wings and Water

Iggy stands by the glass wall on the second floor, staring out at the corporate campus with a barely perceptible grin. He sees me approach and beckons me over.

"Check out the reflecting pond." He points to the ornamental pool running between two buildings. It's less than a foot deep, surrounded by shrubs on the long sides and winding paths leading to the narrow ends where people can admire the landscaped beauty of the company's vast campus. And on a day like today, some of the researchers have taken a few minutes after lunch to sit by the edge and dangle their feet in the cool water, occasionally splashing to let their inner children play.

I poke my elbow at Iggy, whose smile is even broader now. "I can tell you want to play. Nothing going on this afternoon. Go on down and have some fun."

"I was just there. Blue was trying to get Wings into the water. It was pretty funny."

Blue loves the water, and she likes to go there after lunch to sit and read technical papers. She even has the unfortunate habit of throwing the papers in the water when the work annoys her. Then she splashes through the pool chasing the pages, jumping on them aggressively and cursing the paper's author. If there's a dry paper in her office, it must be technically sound.

I'm less sure about Wings, who I can't remember ever being by the pool. He immigrated from Czechoslovakia a few years ago and still has a strong Eastern European accent. When he doesn't like something, you can hear him shouting in multiple languages from a great distance.

"So, did Blue get him in the water? I don't see him."

Iggy laughs. "Not a chance. Wings doesn't do water. Says it reminds him of how he escaped to the west. Apparently, he snuck out of Czechoslovakia in the tank of a water truck. Spent nearly a day sloshing in the dark and wet to escape to America. Promises he'll never go in water again."

I haven't heard this story about Wings, but it doesn't surprise me that Iggy knows it, since the two of them are in the lab's band, The Dead Snails. Iggy plays lead guitar and Wings is the drummer.

"Given such a background, I'd say Blue won't be getting Wings in the water, will she?"

"Not likely. When we rehearse, Wings doesn't say much. He's the only one in the band who doesn't do any singing. Just drums and drums and drums. Doesn't even stop between songs, just keeps the beat going and shouts, 'Next song. Let's go. Next song.' But last night, he had a little more to say, and it was not very nice to Blue."

"She's dialing up the pressure, eh?"

Iggy nods. "Way high. She's decided that it's her mission in life to get Wings in the water. Promised him yesterday that she'd make it happen somehow. Wings is not happy."

That night, I catch Blue as we're leaving the building, so I bring up the subject. She beams and leads me outside. When we're away from any other people, she stops and explains.

"I'm going to get Wings in that water tomorrow after lunch. You know he's got a best-paper award in his office, and he waves it around whenever anybody says his English is poor. 'I write paper!' he likes to shout. 'I write good!' He's right, of course, because that paper really is clever. As you'd expect, it reads like a foreigner wrote it, but nobody cares. Anyway, I'm going to use that award to get him in the water."

I can see where this is headed. "You're going to toss it in the pool and make him get it?"

"Yep. I've promised him that he'll be in the water tomorrow, and he will." She opens her messenger bag and shows me the best-paper award that she's already taken from Wings's office. "Be at the pool tomorrow after lunch."

I'm amused by this challenge, and I hope Wings survives.

The next morning, as I enter the building, Wings is already heading out. I doubt he's been there all night because his clothes look fresh and his hair is as neatly groomed as ever. But he's in a hurry to get somewhere and doesn't stop to chat. He might have noticed the missing award, or he might not and is merely moving at his usual energetic and determined speed. It's hard to tell with Wings.

After lunch, I wander out to the reflecting pool, curious to see what will happen. Blue and Wings are there, arguing by the edge of the water, and a larger than usual crowd has gathered to watch.

"You're going in now, Wings, just like I promised."

"I *not* going in. You wrong. You take my award. Give it back!"

"OK, here it is." She pulls it from her bag, and before Wings can grab it, she flings it into the pool. "Go fetch."

It's a clear-plastic plaque, so it should float and will certainly not be damaged by the water. I would expect Wings to be very upset by this, but strangely, he isn't.

Instead, he turns to watch, a light smirk on his face as his award arcs through the air.

When the plaque hits the water, it lands without noise. I was prepared for a splash, but Blue threw it pretty far, so perhaps the ambient bustle of Silicon Valley has overpowered this minor sound. Then I notice something even stranger. The award is indeed floating, but it's not bobbing up and down. It's on *top* of the water, not a trace of it submerged. And no ripples emanate as it perches completely still in the pool.

I turn to look at Wings, but he's gone, walking down the long side to where his award waits peacefully. Then he steps into the water to fetch it. But when his foot hits the surface, the entire pool depresses under his shoe, as if it's covered in plastic. When he puts all his weight on his foot, the water seems to tear open and wiggles a little as he takes the next step. It looks like it's made of rubber. Wings grabs his award from the surface and walks back, shaking globs of clear goo from his feet. All of us stand by the pool, squinting hard at what we thought was liquid.

Wings returns to Blue and pushes her into the pool. Given how shallow it is, this might normally injure her. But she merely bounces on the surface as if she's on a trampoline.

"What did you do?" she calls as she peels her arm from the sticky surface.

"I buy buckets of gelatin and dump in pool. Now water harder, and I don't get wet."

Getting Rid of the Car

Ah, how the mighty can fall, even when they are renowned automobiles. This little car was once famous, used in advertising for years and known all over the tech world. A dark blue sub-compact with red and white stripes running from nose to tail, it seats two and has a bubble-shaped body with amusingly tiny tires. This is one cute car, which is what made it perfect for company ads.

While the ads ran, the car was parked inside the headquarters building, prominently displayed in the main entrance lobby. Velvet ropes discouraged children from playing on it, because it's that darned cute. But now the ads have stopped, and no amount of adorable is going to save the car, which means it has to leave the lobby. Luckily, the subject of what to do with the car makes it to the executive level, being something of a corporate concern, and that's where Uncle Pavel, our lab director, sees this dilemma as a true goldmine.

Uncle Pavel has a problem. Our lab is nearly out of space, and he craves the adjoining wing of the building that has a large workroom and a half dozen offices. The wing is currently occupied by others in the corporation, but they're getting moved. Uncle Pavel would love very much to take over those offices, but Thomas, Uncle Pavel's boss, refuses to give it to us. He claims the workroom would be wasted on us since we don't have any projects that need such a large space. And that's why a car, even one this small, is ideal.

Within days, Uncle Pavel creates a new research project to experiment with computers in cars. His proposal notes that the company's famous car is being moved away from the main entrance lobby, so he suggests they put it in the workroom. It's a clever cover for needing that much space since any true automotive effort will need bulky tools and supplies that can easily fill the room.

At first, Thomas balks because he really doesn't want to give us the wing, so Uncle Pavel goes straight to the top and informs the executive committee that he needs the car for advanced automotive-computer research. Management wants the car gone, but they don't want anything bad to happen to it, which might cause negative blowback to the company's reputation, so keeping it in-house makes sense. They also like the idea of putting it in their research lab because both the car and the lab are destinations used by corporate PR people to entertain important visitors, and now they can pack two dazzling tech destinations in a single place.

Thomas gets onboard, and the empty wing is handed over to us. The workroom is surprisingly cavernous, now that the former tenants have emptied it so thoroughly. The next day, the famous little car drives down the halls and squeezes through the doors. It's tucked in a corner, and the rest of the space quickly fills with people and their work. We don't mind having the car because honestly, it's cute. Little has changed in that department.

To prove that we really are using the car and the workroom, Uncle Pavel directs The Mountain to write a technical report on possible avenues for automated automobiles. The result is a document so vague, it could have been written at the end of a long evening at Antonio's Nut House, where beer flows, noise is loud, and coherent thought is rare. The document may be insipid, but it belays any doubts that the car is in the right place, so it achieves its goal.

Unfortunately, nothing stays the same in the tech world, and six months later, it's our lab's turn to get moved. Sadly, the new space is much smaller, so we no longer have the luxury of housing a useless car. After a long run of loving devotion, the car must go.

Uncle Pavel explains the issues at our lab meeting. The car can't be driven on the road because it's not insured. Also, there are doubts about whether it can pass inspection without incurring additional costs, so we can't make it road-worthy without spending money, which the company refuses to do. Some folks in the lab would love to drive this little baby, and they're willing to pay the necessary costs. But this isn't going to happen either because the company would have to transfer title, something corporate bean-counters see as compensation, and that would stir up more tax and financial issues which, once again, the company refuses to do.

We sit around the table for a while and conclude that the only option is to destroy the car as cheaply as possible. Nobody wants to give it to a junkyard because that's unimaginative and unworthy of the little icon. Something more creative is necessary. Ideas get thrown around and the discussion gets heated.

After an hour of wasted time, I've heard enough. "Why don't we have a contest? Everyone can make suggestions about how to deal with the car, and we'll go with the winning recommendation."

"Sure." Uncle Pavel shrugs. "As long as I get to decide who wins."

Everyone is tired of the subject, so they agree to the contest. Over the next week, a handful of ideas gets floated, and at the following lab meeting, Uncle Pavel announces his decision.

"OK, people, I got three suggestions about what to do with the car. The first is to drive it into the parking lot and let everyone attack it with whatever tools they can bring. We can scavenge parts from it, then we'll take the rest to a recycler. The only cost is our time spent beating on a car instead of doing real work."

Everyone finds this suggestion to be marginally acceptable, but they were hoping for something more imaginative than a bashfest, so Uncle Pavel moves on to the next suggestion.

"This one has a bit of class to it. Hang the car upside down from the ceiling of our new conference room."

Pizza Man rolls his eyes and gazes at the ceiling. "Why would we want to do that?"

"Well, see ..." Give Me All What We Have explains, revealing himself to be the one who came up with this idea. "It's pretty nice-looking, so I figured we'd enjoy having it mounted on the ceiling. Something fun to remind us of the little car that could. Plus, it won't take up any valuable floor space."

Mr. Rogers glances up with a frown. "What if it falls on us?"

Uncle Pavel waves that one away. "First of all, nobody will sit under it. The suggestion is to mount it above the table, so if it falls, the table will catch it. And we'll remove the engine and anything heavy before doing this, so it's just a shell."

We discuss this a bit more, but Uncle Pavel finally quashes the idea. "All good, people, but there are two problems. First, this is going to cost, to gut the car and to mount it on the ceiling. The company doesn't really want to spend that kind of money, as I've already made clear. But second and much more important, the new building managers won't allow us to do custom stuff like that. So we can't do this, and we're going with suggestion number three."

"Excellent!" Boom shakes a fist, no doubt because he has won the contest.

Uncle Pavel nods at Boom and smiles. "That's right, I like your idea best. Go ahead and tell everyone."

Boom leaps to his feet. "It's simple. We're going to blow up the car."

This evokes wide eyes and dropped jaws all around. I know how much Boom likes explosives. The lab even gave him this nickname because of it. But blowing up a car? This sounds like a dangerous proposition. Boom explains how he's going to *safely* blow up the car.

"Most of you know that we go down to the California desert every year to race our motorcycles. Well, there are some very remote places, far from anything. I'm going to rent a backhoe—on my own nickel so the lab doesn't have to pay anything. I'll drive it and the car out to the desert, dig a pit, put the car in, cover it with sand, then blow it sky high. We can watch from a safe distance and record it on video. It's going to be bomb-a-rific!"

Suddenly, the wide eyes in the room are accompanied by broad smiles. It's still a crazy idea, but now everyone likes it. A lot. We're going to blow up the iconic corporate car, which has all sorts of subversive overtones.

It takes Boom a while to get this organized. Uncle Pavel gives him the pink slip so he can drive the car away, warning him to load it on a trailer soon because it's still not insured.

Boom heads down to the Southern California desert a few days early with a trailer containing the car and a backhoe. Two days later, a caravan of lab people journeys south to watch the event.

When we arrive, the pit has been dug, and the car is in it. The pit is quite deep, at least ten feet down to the roof of the car. When I stand at the edge, I can see the familiar red and white stripes, my last visit with the fun little toy. Once everyone shows up, Boom gets into his earth-mover and covers the car, making the ground level again—only a single wire emerges. He then moves the backhoe to safety and connects the wire to a detonating plunger. This cute little car will soon be toast.

The lab gathers at a safe distance and starts the cameras. Boom leads a ten-second countdown, more enthusiastic than any New Year's celebration. When we get to zero, he throws himself on the plunger and I watch a huge dome of earth bubble up to the tune of an ear-splitting roar. It settles back down in a depressed crater, and a small dark cloud billows out, spraying a fine mist of sand accompanied by a harsh burning odor. A spectacular explosion, for sure.

Boom returns to the scene with the backhoe so he can smooth out the ground, then we load up everything and drive home. The car is gone, pulverized into little pieces, and buried where nobody will find it again. Problem solved.

But a month later, I'm in Boom's office, and the subject of the car comes up. He closes the door and beckons me over to his computer. "Check this out." He shows me a video of the little corporate car driving around a small town. It parks outside a grocery store and a young couple get out to go shopping.

I give Boom the stink eye. "Is this an old video?"

"Nope." Boom grins. "This was taken last week."

"Wait! Is this really the company car?" The stripe is familiar, but there could be many others with that paint job.

"The very same." Boom chuckles. "I gave it to my brother-in-law and he loves it."

I'm curious now. "So ... What *did* we blow up?"

"Oh, that." Boom waves it away. "I found it at a junkyard, completely worthless, even the engine was gone. But it had the same rounded roof, which is all anyone could see after I painted stripes and buried it with the explosives. That's what we blew up."

Punk Superiority

Punk rock is emerging these days, and nerds are in love. It's rock-and-roll played fast, loud, and hard, with lyrics so intensely disturbing that anyone taking them seriously becomes agitated. Those who understand the satiric slant, however, recognize this as nothing more than the latest in folk music.

Around the lab, there are several punk fans, particularly Peter Sanders, who gave himself the nickname Punk Pete so everyone would know his dedication to the cause. Punk Pete is slim and average-height with a dark, receding hairline. He's always neatly dressed, even in this new punk phase where his black outfits are accessorized with skull-and-crossbones rings, padlocks on his belt loops, and a necklace made from heavy rusted chain. If I didn't already know him as good old Peter Sanders, I'd certainly wonder about this harshly transformed nerd.

Another significant punk influencer is Wild Man Matt, who was given that name some time ago, before we were aware of punk. His real name is Matt Steele, a tall nerd with long scraggly hair who programs in the lab. A former Vietnam veteran, Wild Man Matt has clearly taken too many drugs and now stares blankly much of the time, leading one to think he's permanently high.

Anyone into the music scene in Palo Alto knows the place to hear new acts is The Edge, a club in town that brings some serious noise. They usually finish their gigs by 1 or 2 in the morning, after which people wander the mostly dead suburban streets looking for something else to do. The shop where everyone ends up is The Creamery, the only all-night restaurant, where they may not serve alcohol, but the milkshakes are stellar, and the smell of French fries intensifies the late-night hunger.

I'm at The Creamery one night after another fine evening of jarring entertainment. My head feels like it's wrapped in cotton, and my ears are still ringing from the pounding of the music. Other voices are dim echoes as if we're talking through a tin-can telephone.

But there's nothing wrong with my eyes, so I notice Wild Man Matt as soon as he walks in the door. He's got his signature duster coat—years before *The Matrix* will make it popular—long, black, and swirling around his legs as he strides purposefully past the booths. Before he can get to my table, he spots familiar people, gives two of them a wraparound hug, then takes a seat. He's a fixture at The Creamery, and he knows nearly everyone here, so he'll work the booths, stopping to sit with everyone and eventually get to me. Eager to say hi, I get up and walk over.

When I arrive at the table where Wild Man Matt is sitting, I'm surprised to see Punk Pete there. It's no shock to see Punk Pete at The Creamery because he probably saw the same show and is seeking the same late-night sugar rush to help digest the music. But what surprises me is that Wild Man Matt stopped at this table. I happen to know these two punk aficionados aren't very good friends. Punk Pete thinks Wild Man Matt is a damaged loser who isn't really punk, just brain dead. Wild Man Matt, who's less brain-dead than he sometimes appears, thinks Punk Pete is a poser, someone who pretends to be punk but is only into the fashion. I hear them complain about each other quite often at work, so I'm surprised to see them having a friendly discussion about the performance we've just seen.

I turn to head back to my table because Wild Man Matt took the last free seat, and there's no more room in this booth. But before I get far, Wild Man Matt shouts loud enough to pierce the fog.

"You! You!" he stands and points at Punk Pete. "You're just ..." He pauses to think about what Punk Pete is; his over-drugged mind either running at high speed or stalled by the side of the road, it's hard to say. After a few seconds, he finishes his thought. "You can't buy punk."

This is very true, both in general and specifically in the case of Punk Pete. He does try to buy his attitude. Sure, he wears black all the time, but if you look closely, his clothes are top quality—high-thread-count slacks with silk shirts—not very punk. On top of that, he's always coming into work with punk stuff to give away so everyone else knows he cares. I've gotten records, posters, little pins with punk sayings, and T-shirts for obscure punk bands. This is one nerd who loves to spread the wealth.

For all the money he spends, Punk Pete has the surprising counterpoint of being cheap. Given that he makes a nice salary at the lab, it's ridiculous to hear him pretend to be poor. But he likes to regale the lab with his skinflint stories, such as how he goes to Hobees for the salad-bar dinner and does his very best to make sure the one plate he's given holds at least two plates worth of food. He starts by lining the plate with lettuce, sticking far over the edges so the plate is suddenly bigger. Then he piles that with food, organizing it so the heavier items sit lower on the plate to form a solid foundation for the fluffier foods that can then pile high. His outrage at getting caught by management and asked not to eat there anymore elicits no sympathy around the lab. Pay for your damned food!

After Wild Man Matt's outburst, Punk Pete works through a host of facial expressions, finally settling on a scowl. "*You* clearly haven't bought punk. You don't even like the Sex Pistols, the greatest punk band in the world."

Wild Man Matt shrugs. "Sex Pistols are OK, but they got too famous, so now everyone wants to be like them."

"Everyone wants to be like them?" Punk Pete slaps hands to the side of his face, Munch-scream style. "Their lead singer committed suicide. How punk is that? No other band has copied that."

"Ouccchhh!" Wild Man Matt waves this away. "He didn't commit suicide, he ODed on drugs. Everyone does that … Hendrix, Joplin. It doesn't make him punk, just fucked up."

"Oh yeah?" Punk Pete gets to his feet so he can face Wild Man Matt directly. "Who's more punk than Sex Pistols?"

"Oh, let's see …" Wild Man Matt looks to the ceiling for a few seconds, then breaks out in a broad smile. "How about Diamanda Galás? Now *she's* punk! Have you heard her album, *The Litanies of Satan*?"

Punk Pete furrows his brow. "I haven't heard of her. But I'm sure the Sex Pistols are every bit as punk."

At this point, the two of them notice Standard in the next booth, who is watching their argument with an amused look. As the lead singer of the lab band, The Dead Snails, he's a prime target, and both Punk Pete and Wild Man Matt demand his opinion. Who is more punk, they want to know, Sex Pistols or Diamanda Galás?

Standard settles the argument easily. "Both great." Then he pops another French fry into his mouth.

Punk Pete can't let it go and insists on an answer, so Standard considers for a while.

"Well, Sex Pistols are good because they're more accessible and have influenced more punk bands, but Diamanda Galás is good because she spends an entire side of an album screaming, something I couldn't do if I tried." Standard refuses to say any more, and the two combatants soon disperse in the late-night crowd.

But over the next week, Punk Pete goes on the offense, promoting Sex Pistols every chance he gets. He even buys all their albums to decorate the lunch room walls. Wild Man Matt keeps it simple, maintaining Diamanda Galás is better and that is all there is to it.

But Punk Pete needs an answer. He corners the members of The Dead Snails one day at lunch. Standard is there, as well as Iggy the guitarist, Boom the bass player, and Wings the drummer. Punk Pete demands to know who they think is more punk. The four of them discuss this among themselves, failing to reach a consensus. But they do offer a cryptic answer to Punk Pete. The band is playing a party in two weeks, and they promise to announce a decision at the gig, telling their audience exactly who they think commands punk superiority. This mollifies Punk Pete, and he leaves them in peace.

Two weeks later, I'm at a party hosted by Blue, who loves to have live bands play at her bashes. Everyone knows about the battle of the punk bands, and they're curious to know whether the lab band will tell us that Sex Pistols rule or Diamanda Galás. The party is in full swing when the band emerges in a corner of the room where their equipment awaits. Wings climbs into his drum kit, Iggy and Boom strap on guitars, and Standard grabs a microphone.

"OK, people." His amplified voice silences the room. "We're The Dead Snails, and we command you to dance!" With that, the band breaks into their first song, and everyone at the party obeys.

After two chest-pounding songs, Standard brings up the issue we're all waiting to hear. "So there seems to be a little competition in the lab, and folks want to know who is more punk, Sex Pistols or Diamanda Galás. We wanted to play a song by both groups, but in the end, we decided to play only one band's music, and here it is."

This is what everyone wants to know, the answer to the fleeting and largely irrelevant question of punkness. Wings clicks his drumsticks to count in the song, then the entire band enters for a rousing performance of "Pretty Vacant," a classic Sex Pistols song. Everyone starts to dance, happy to hear that Sex Pistols rule. Most of the members of the lab don't even know the works of Diamanda Galás, so this seems like the obvious choice. I pogo across the floor and join in the chorus, singing along with Standard when he bellows, "We're so pretty, oh so pretty . . . Vacant! And we don't care."

Punk Pete is in heaven, running around to everyone on the dance floor to brag, "I told you so." Wild Man Matt isn't there, and I find him outside on the deck, passing a joint in the brisk air. He exhales a smoke-filled hit and denies any possibility that Punk Pete knows a damned thing.

"I don't care. I don't even care about the Sex Pistols."

I take a hit from his joint. "But you care about Diamanda Galás."

"I do care about her, but then again, I don't." He giggles. "I really don't care about anything, you know."

"You don't care that Punk Pete has been needling you for weeks?"

Wild Man Matt doesn't even care about that. "I'm quitting next month. I've made enough money for a while, so I can go back to the city and hang with my real friends." I know all about this because he's told me about his true goal in life: to not work. He spends about nine months of every year on the streets of San Francisco, hanging with the homeless people in the worst areas of the city and getting by with the secret stash he's earned during the other three months. He likes to joke that he's a homeless person with an ATM card.

I have to admit Wild Man Matt is right; none of this matters. Who in their proper punk mind would give two shits or even one. Nobody, that's who. Except perhaps Punk Pete, who clearly cares too much.

I return to the dance floor as the band wraps up a song and Standard is about to introduce the next one. But instead of a brief segue, he decides to pontificate some more.

"You know, people, Sex Pistols are truly awesome. And I bet most of you haven't even heard Diamanda Galás. But let me tell you, she's much more awesome. She is the soul of punk, a true goddess, and if we could scream like her, we would have done one of her songs. But she's entirely too amazing for our pathetic band. So, if you want to know who is more punk, well, she is. Hands down. But if you need catchy tunes to keep you jumping all night, you'll have to settle for Sex Pistols."

Punk Pete howls so loudly that I wonder if he's singing a Diamanda Galás song, but he's just in pain, perhaps for the first time in his life.

Management

I've known Leap for many years, going back to high school when we called him by his given name, Jason Hawk. A tall Texas nerd with glasses, a wide face, and a goofy grin, he's one of the smartest in the lab, but he speaks so seldom and so quietly that few realize they're in the presence of greatness. His nickname is Leap because he was born on February 29, back in 1952, and has yet to celebrate his tenth birthday. Thanks to some interesting coincidences as well as the small number of people doing computer research these days, the two of us keep running into each other, and we're currently employed at the same lab.

Right now, Leap's project is the darling of mysterious upper-level oracles entrusted with predicting the future of computing, so they've elevated him to a management role with real humans at his command. The buzz around the lab is he's a rising star, but he's new at this, so his chances for success are still unknown. I wish him well, but I don't envy the hours he'll waste drafting tedious documents, sitting through pointless meetings, and dealing with pathetic whiners both above and below his grade. So far, he's undaunted because nobody's whining yet, and the boosts of encouragement he gets make him believe the job is simple and solvable.

But today, the rising star appears to have hit his first cloud. He's standing in the doorway to my office rocking from side to side, hands clasping then unclasping, flickering his gaze my way but unable to connect. I watch his nervous display for an uncomfortable few seconds.

"OK, get in here. Have a seat." I motion to the small sofa I keep handy. It barely fits in my tiny office, but it's a great place to fold up and crash when pulling an all-nighter, as many in the lab know first hand.

Leap glances at the sofa then shakes his head. "No, I need a little more privacy than that. Can we go somewhere obscure for lunch?"

I'm a sucker for private gossip, and Leap clearly has a secret to tell, so I suggest a new restaurant that few of our colleagues have discovered. "Have you been to Brown Rice? It's a tiny sushi place that just opened."

Leap's eyes shine. "Yes, perfect. Just heard about it last week. Come on!"

"Whoa, give me five." I turn back to my screen, but his mood has pushed my current thread of activity below the level needed to focus right now, so I turn back to him with a smirk. "Never mind. Squeet." Leap understands this Southern-California slang for "Let's go eat."

As soon as Leap settles in my passenger seat, he groans from the comfort of the warm car, although this could possibly be the temporary relief from whatever demons are infecting his head. I give him a moment to relax as I navigate the parking lot and make my way down the sunny streets of Palo Alto.

It doesn't take him long to start talking. "You know how I'm running a team now. Got five programmers and even a project manager who works with me to make sure it goes well. It's all kinds of fine, but B.M. wants results and at the same time is trying to take one of my programmers off the project."

There's always trouble when you have to deal with B.M., an upper-level manager who runs several of the teams in the lab. He reports directly to Uncle Pavel, so he's near the top of the food-chain around here. Some claim they call him B.M. because he's a Boss Man, but others—who find him thoroughly distasteful—insist it stands for something more reminiscent of fecal matter. He's one of the main reasons I refuse to do any management, so I offer a light laugh over Leap's trouble.

"That'll teach you to do useful work. Next time, stick to obscure research that nobody cares about. Besides, you have your own cheerleader now. You should send Slick in to do battle." Slick is Leap's product manager, a man whose real name no one can remember because he's such a slime-dog that even *he* goes by Slick. He's always looking for a big venture that'll make him millions. He may be annoying, but at least he makes projects happen. Leap only wanted three programmers on his team, but Slick got him five, so if B.M. is on the warpath, Slick is the man to call.

"Maybe." Leap shrugs. "But Slick isn't what you think. In fact, he's been working against the project from the start. He's not going to help me keep my people."

"Slick is against the project? What kind of project manager hates his own project?"

Leap sighs. "Let me tell you a story. When I got the team last month, they also gave me Slick. He's done a number of projects around the company and everyone at the home office loves him. I thought he'd be great for my project. But on the first day we met, I was sitting in the meeting room early, too excited to do much else. Slick was the second to arrive, and he didn't know who I was, so just for fun, I told him I was one of the programmers, not the team leader. I wanted to get to know him as a colleague instead of as his boss."

"Wait, how does that make sense? You obviously knew who he was because you saw his photo in the company directory. How come he didn't do the same and know who you were?"

Leap chuckles. "That's Slick for you. Anyway, we're sitting there, the only ones in the room, so he looks around to make sure nobody's listening, then he pulls me close and tells me he can't wait for the project to fail. The way he figures it, each job he does advances him up the corporate ladder to bigger projects and higher pay, so he tries to be done with them as soon as possible to move on and up. Then he informs me that the best way to finish work on a project is for it to fail because if it's a success, he'll have to waste years on it, but failure happens faster."

I give Leap a look of disgust. "He really said that? I bet he was surprised when he found out you're running the show."

"Yeah, a bit embarrassing. He made up for it by forcing B.M. to give us two more programmers. That was pretty nice."

I arch an eyebrow. "I don't know, Leap. Slick may be trying to kill your project sooner by raising the costs. With two extra programmers, you're gobbling budget at a faster rate. It would explain why B.M. wants to trim you back; the expense could tank the project. You really ought to take a cue from Slick and learn how to play this game."

"So, it's a game, is it?"

We've arrived at the restaurant, so I fold my arms. "You know it is, and you can't win if you don't play." Few nerds care for sports or sports metaphors, but sometimes they're apt.

Leap tightens his mouth. "Well, all I know is I've got a meeting with B.M. after lunch to try to save my best programmer. She's really sharp and, honestly, I'd rather lose the other four." Leap shakes his head. "It's not looking good." He continues to grumble as we enter the restaurant, and he grouses about lab politics for the entire meal.

An hour after lunch, he's back in my office, now sporting an unsteady smile, his brow furrowed as if he's trying to remember something simple and is kicking himself for forgetting. I point to the sofa, and he closes the door before taking a seat. I'm not sure what's going on, but I've got to know. The code I'm debugging is surprisingly resistant, so I save my work and prepare myself for the news.

Leap lets out a long breath. "You told me to play the game, but I just couldn't do it."

"So ... You lost her?"

"Well, it went like this. B.M. brought in two of his managers, me and Acre, who it turns out also has five people on his team. Then he told us that he has to let one person go, and it's either my best programmer or one of Acre's. He gave us his usual smug look and invited us to make our best pitch in the hopes that our people would survive the cut."

"Ouch. And people wonder why I don't want to do management." I can see how this battle between Leap and Acre is going to hurt. Acre's name is Hector Leblanc, a thin, balding, and bearded Canadian from Quebec. Because he speaks French, the lab took to calling him Hectare, pronounced with an exaggerated second syllable, and that quickly transformed to a different measure of land, Acre.

Concerned about Leap's prospects, I offer encouragement. "You know, this is a situation where the game is vitally important."

"Yes, I know." Leap exhales. "I was sitting there staring at Acre, thinking that I had to fight him for my team. I had to boast about the significance of my work, explain why it's superior to Acre's unworthy effort, and support it with statistics, projections, and bullet points. Acre would do the same to me, which would bloody us both, then B.M. would make his decision. It's disgusting."

I nod. "That's management for you. Get used to it."

Leap shakes his head. "The thing is, I like Acre. I don't want him to hate me. And I knew that no matter how this meeting ended, one of us was going to be mad at the other, when in truth, we should be mad at B.M. The situation made me see the insanity of it, how B.M. had rephrased the meeting so that Acre and I were the ones at fault, not him. And it dawned on me that this was not a simple game with understandable rules. It's war. It's chaos. It's the Roman fucking coliseum, and B.M. was the emperor, watching as Acre and I gear up to do battle. I could practically taste the bile as it rose from my gut, that's how much I loathe this game."

"But what choice do you have? If you want to save your people, you've got to do battle." I sympathize with Leap, because Acre really is a nice guy with an interesting project.

Leap frowns. "Well, I knew I had to play the game, but I also knew—if this was like other management games—the outcome was preordained, and the carnage was merely show. So before the lions could be let out of their cages, I tried to handle it with less blood."

I sit up straight at this notion. "Less blood? How was that possible when someone was about to lose their head?"

"I didn't know for sure, but I felt like I had to try. I told B.M. that this was *his* job, not ours. That my project could not be compared with Acre's, and that it was not my role to criticize Acre's work. I probably raised my voice a little as I vented exasperation. Then I finished by telling B.M. that if he needed to cut someone, *he* would have to be the one to do it, not me and not Acre. Finally, I sat back and glared at him, wishing I could go home and end this stupid day."

I shake my head slowly, mourning the passing of Leap who may not be as much of a rising star as everyone thinks. "Oh well, I hear SunTex is hiring."

"No, you don't get it." Leap raises a hand to his forehead. "After my outburst, B.M. agreed that his demand was unfair and accepted that he had to make the decision, not me and not Acre. Then he paused for a second and announced his answer. Acre's project will lose a programmer, not mine."

"What? You went to your boss, told him to fuck off, and he did?"

"I know! Could it be that the right way to play this game is from the sidelines?"

Lucky Snake

There's a big crowd gathered around the table in the conference room, cheering enthusiastically. Between cheers, I can hear Snake's clipped British accent, explaining technical details. He's quite smart and knows all sorts of information, from math and computer graphics to the proper way to make tea and the most efficient way to kill someone with a garrote. The tea brewing is something you'd expect, given his posh accent, but his perfectly calm explanation of more grisly topics always takes me by surprise. He may talk like James Bond, but his stout and balding appearance doesn't sell the image. Few can anticipate the thoughts percolating in Snake's head.

Today, he's demonstrating his latest project, a robot snake. He's been talking about this for so long that he's earned his nickname, and now he's driving home the moniker by bringing his creation to work. Snakes, he explains, are simple creatures where each segment follows the one ahead of it. The serpentine motion of the body comes naturally when the head moves left and right. For months now, he's been telling us about his night-time hobby of building this mechanical reptile in his garage. Each motorized segment moves forward, guided by the one ahead of it. Today, his cyber pet is ready to slither for us.

"Snakes can have hundreds of segments, but this little fellow has only fifty." He pats the diamond-painted head that sports an anthropomorphic smile, then he clicks a remote control to steer the head from side to side. The creature wriggles across the table in perfect snake-like motion, and the crowd applauds the tiny beast.

Snake is really Milton Garvey, a graphics researcher who programs the most fascinating imagery. One of his programs lets you draw a curve that gets folded, tapered, and squiggled into a most ornate decoration, reminiscent of European Rococo extravagances. Everyone in the lab is using his program to create pretty designs for their papers in a well-intentioned but ultimately futile attempt to add some class.

Another of Snake's graphic creations is, of course, a snake animation. Before making his motorized creature, he programmed a cartoon one slithering across the sand. Once he'd proved that realistic snake motion could be made this way, he was ready to build his little toy, which consumed hundreds of dollars and the same number of hours.

Snake concludes his demonstration by talking about the next one he plans to build, with an infrared sensor in the head. His little heat-seeking snake will mimic the sidewinder, a clever reptile that finds its prey by sensing body heat. Snake quickly adds more of his arcane weapons knowledge by explaining how the sidewinder heat-seeking missile was given that name because of the snake. If computers hadn't come along to distract him, Snake would be a very dangerous man.

A few weeks later, Snake sits quietly at the lunch table, his mouth tight and his eyes refusing to focus. It's unlike him to avoid conversation, especially since everyone is talking about the latest action movie, and I'm sure Snake has some opinions on the film.

During a lull in the chatter, I turn to him. "You're quiet, Snake. What's going on?"

He draws in a long breath and blows out a sorry sigh. "I'm quitting. Sorry, folks, but this is goodbye."

Everyone at the lunch table gasps and wants to know where he's going. SunTex has been our main competition, but Snake isn't going there. Nor is he going to Park Ex, another powerhouse in the Valley. With each new company name someone offers, he shakes his head. Finally, I consider broader possibilities.

"Are you joining the CIA? Perhaps MI5?" Snake's arcane weapons knowledge would make him a perfect spook.

But Snake laughs. "Don't I wish. The company I'm going to isn't a spy agency, and it doesn't do computers." But when asked, he refuses to give the company's name. All he'll say is that it's here in the valley, so he'll still be around. Then, he switches gears.

"I was working in my garage last week, finally got the infrared sensor in the snake's head. My little sidewinder was slithering all over the floor, following me as I moved. I was having fun running around and making it find me. I also programmed the head so if it hit something, it would move left or right to try and keep going. The garage is pretty cluttered, but my new toy kept seeking me out, which is awesome.

"I decided to give it a challenge and hide in a corner, with plenty of clutter in between, to see how long it would take to work around all the junk and get to me. At that moment, my neighbor came over to borrow a garden tool. She's borrowed tools before, so she called a hello to me, and I called out to her from my hiding place in the garage. I heard her pulling a shovel from my pile of tools, then I heard her scream. Before I could get to her, she had whacked the poor beast multiple times. Like a real snake, one whack wouldn't stop it because all the little segment motors kept moving, so it writhed like a living serpent as she beat the life out of it."

"Oh, hell!" I'm horrified to think of this delicate creation being bashed with a shovel. "Can you repair it?"

"Not a chance. By the time it stopped wiggling, she'd crushed it completely. When I got to her, she was bent over, staring at the wires coming out of it and scratching her head. I, of course, was in shock to see my baby so thoroughly dead.

"I spent the next half hour explaining my snake while she apologized pitifully. Finally, I couldn't take any more of her sympathy, so I sent her away with my shovel and went inside to drown my sorrows in cheap red wine."

Snake told a sad story, but I still don't understand why he's leaving the lab. "Are you quitting because of this? Is that why you're not going to do computer research anymore? Don't let this ruin your life."

"Oh, that's not it at all." Snake chuckles lightly. "Turns out my neighbor's husband is the CEO of a huge toy company. A few months ago, they decided to build a research lab to explore computerized toys, but they had no idea who could run it. When he heard about my snake, he rushed over and insisted I be the lab director. How could I refuse? So now I'll have lots of people working for me, and I'll get paid to build robot snakes."

Doves and Hawks

The most popular Chinese restaurant in Palo Alto is The Little, which lives up to its name by occupying a tiny slot on University Avenue between two larger stores. The food is outrageously spicy, which appeals to nerds so much that one of them took a job there as a waiter.

The classic story about The Little concerns a computer salesman from the East Coast who was dining there with a Stanford professor one night. They got into an argument about some minor technical detail, and when they couldn't agree, the professor suggested they ask the waiter. The salesman scoffed at the notion, but when they finally did query the waiter, his instant and precise answer flabbergasted the poor salesman and left him stunned by Palo Alto, a town where even the waiters are nerds.

Unable to resist their Kung Pao chicken and orange peel beef, I'm dining at The Little and notice four very unusual people at a nearby table. They're all nerds who love the food here, but I didn't think they loved each other. Two of them work at companies that do secret government projects, and the other two are ultraliberal peaceniks. Yet there they are, dining and chatting happily.

It's no surprise that the US military has jumped on the computer craze. When students graduate with advanced degrees, they're often courted by these organizations, and the salaries they're promised are always much better than what commercial corporations offer. The downside is the workers will never be able to tell anyone what they're doing, and they'll certainly not be publishing or going to conferences anymore. If you want the extra bump in salary, your research career is officially over.

I haven't seen much of the two people at the next table who opted for dark computing at WP, the local house of cyber spies. They still live in the valley, but they don't hang out in the same circles anymore. One of them is Daria Thornberg, known to one and all as Darth. Tall with short dark hair, she never had many words to offer before taking a job at WP, and now she has even fewer. I once asked her what she did there, and she said she'd be glad to tell me on my last day in hospice.

The other renegade to the dark side is Ross Bengal, a stocky man who loves basketball and has earned the nickname Hook for his great hook shots. Hook is chatty enough to make up for Darth's reclusiveness, and he often teases her about it, poking and prodding to get even two words out of her mouth. Watching them interact would make you think they're a couple, but nothing could be further from the truth. They're just solid friends.

On the peace-loving side of the table, keeping up their side of the conversation, are a man and woman who are indeed a couple. The man has the nickname Sky for his incredible height, which is nearly six feet, four inches. He's Mack Jensen, and his Scottish good looks and wavy dark hair have caught the attention of many female nerds in the valley. With him is Zoey Peterson, a rugged woman from Alaska who sports straight, dirty-blonde hair and big glasses. She loves anything brightly colored and takes trips to the southwestern desert to see the dazzling hot-air balloon festivals, thus earning herself the nickname Rainbow. Sky and Rainbow show up at war protests, and they're notable for refusing to work on any project that has even the faintest scent of military secrecy. Why are they dining with Darth and Hook?

When dinner is over, Sky and Rainbow leave first. But before they do, they grab a brown paper bag that's been sitting by their feet and discreetly hand it to Darth. She looks inside, wrinkles her nose, then wraps the bag tightly and shoves it in her purse. I have to wonder what sort of gift this might be, eliciting a notably negative reaction from the taciturn Darth.

Sky and Rainbow leave unfinished beers, which I understand because they prefer wine, and The Little doesn't offer any. Now that they're gone, Hook keeps up a running conversation at the table while he scarfs the remaining brew. Darth sits there quietly, offering occasional eye rolls as he drinks and gabs. Finally, they go their separate ways, him to the bathroom for personal beer recycling, her to the exit and merciful freedom from her chatty friend.

I'm at a T-shirt party a few days later at Sky and Rainbow's place. They throw yearly T-shirt events and even award prizes in a number of categories: the most colorful, the funniest, the cleverest, the rudest, and a half-dozen other obscurities. My T-shirt won't win any awards tonight, but it's always fun to see the competitors. At one point in the evening, I corner Rainbow and mention that I saw her and Sky with Darth and Hook.

She blushes. "Yeah, I noticed you. It's not what you think. We're not looking for jobs at WP."

I laugh. "It never crossed my mind that you'd even consider working there. I'm just surprised the four of you were getting along so well. I've heard the screeds you and Sky say about WP, and I assume you've lectured those two about their career choice. But the conversation seemed friendlier than that."

Rainbow pauses, avoiding a response by straightening the plastic silverware on the party's food table. When all the pieces are stacked neatly, she looks back at me, bites her lip, and says something truly surprising. "They tell us secrets about their work."

I blink hard and let my eyes widen. "Won't they have to kill you now?"

Rainbow laughs. "They're not telling us real secrets, just general comments about what it's like to work there. Darth's job is eavesdropping, writing software to monitor emails for classified information. Hook's writing a program to scan immigration records, looking for suspicious foreigners."

"Wow." I can't believe they'd reveal this information. It's not a great surprise the company does this. WP hints broadly about such activity. But hearing confirmation from the workers is still a shock. I lean closer to Rainbow. "What else?"

She flattens her lips and shakes her head. "That's all they'll tell us, but at least we got that much out of them."

"I see. And what are you giving them for this information? They must want something for revealing details even this vague. Russian spies would pay good money to be at the table when the four of you have dinner. And I did notice a payoff at the end of the meal. What's this information costing you?"

Rainbow smiles and nods. "We're paying, but not with money. You have to understand that we like Hook and Darth, and we used to be closer friends. So we've stayed in touch, and we have dinner regularly to catch up. At first, they hardly said a word, but one night they complained about something surprising at work, and we had an instant solution for them. In exchange for this, they agreed to dish a little. We don't want to know actual government secrets, just some insight into their work lives. It's fascinating."

"OK, then. What are you paying for this innocuous information?"

"Um." She reddens slightly. "Piss."

"What?" I snap my head. "There was urine in that paper bag?"

Rainbow shrugs. "WP has random drug testing. The workers have dubbed the company 'WP-in-a-bottle' because they're forced to give urine samples occasionally. Sky and I are drug-free, so we give them clean pee, which they keep in their desks and submit whenever testing gets announced."

Mister Jerk

Mister Jerk comes into my office with his usual arrogance, head high and lips tight on a turned-down mouth to keep his inner disdain at bay. As far as he's concerned, nobody knows more than he does, and few know as much. When someone gives a talk at the lab, Mister Jerk interrupts every other sentence with minor criticisms and almost-intelligent comments. He's been told numerous times to shut the hell up, something people in the lab feel free to say to his face because they know he'll never actually do it.

Naturally, his name isn't Mister Jerk, but instead is Jake Ralston, and as you might expect, Jake doesn't know about his nickname. But Jerk sounds close enough to Jake, so anytime he hears this moniker, he accepts it as a mere mispronunciation. Amusingly, what really bothers Jake Ralston is to be called *mister* since he has a PhD. Generally, most nerds with doctorates ignore the degree, never using the title because it sounds rather pretentious and because nerds are not medical people, so the title is misleading. But Jake loves to call himself doctor and can't wait to brag about his brains. So whenever he hears someone say Mister Jerk, he reminds them that he's *doctor*, completely failing to notice the insult that got delivered.

The women in the lab are particularly incensed with Mister Jerk because he not only thinks he's God's gift to computers, but he also thinks his skill with women is divine. He's an average-looking fellow with short dark hair, a pinched face, and a smile that, when offered, fails to make you feel he cares. At least he's clean and wears a different shirt every day; while that might not be asking much, it isn't universally observed among the nerd community. Still, his reasonable intelligence and absence of foul odors do not compensate for a severe lack of humility.

From what I've heard around the lab, Mister Jerk has asked out nearly every woman here, and most of them grit their teeth when they tell how uncomfortable it is to turn him down. Many of them think jerk isn't a strong enough word to describe him, and some have more colorful language for the man.

One woman in the lab finally said yes, our numerical researcher AP, a short and slender but very intense woman with medium-length brown hair and a hearty laugh for most of life including, apparently, Mister Jerk. Her name is Andrea Pryor, but we use her initials because she no-doubt excelled at AP classes when younger. Brains run in her family—AP's father is a well-respected statistics professor.

Many in the lab seem puzzled by AP's willingness to be with Mister Jerk, but she often has a smile for him when he shows up at a party. Of course, they rarely spend much time together because she runs off whenever he starts to nerd out, which is almost always.

Regardless of my feelings about Mister Jerk, I welcome him when he arrives at my office, and I wait to find out what sort of foolishness he's up to today. He could start one of his lectures, explaining something he thinks I need to know even if I already do, or he might have a nontechnical comment, which could easily turn into a lab meme, another turd of wisdom from Mister Jerk.

Fortunately, his direct and intense style means he doesn't require any prompting to get to the point. "Party! Three weeks from Friday!" He pushes a forceful thumbs-up my way. "It's going to rock so hard that people will be talking about it for months."

I accept his claim of grandeur as a joke and continue the comedy by playing to his massive ego. "Who knows? They may be talking about this party for years. I'm honored to be invited."

My sarcasm barely connects, so Mister Jerk decides to double-down on his generosity in a classic move of his. "My entire women's group will be there, so you should be able to score."

I'm inwardly stunned by the number of red flags in that statement. First, I'm aware of Mister Jerk's presence in a women's group. He didn't start it, so it's certainly not his, as he claims. But as the only man in the group, he presents his membership as proof of his feminist side, then uses it to meet more women. I have to wonder what these women really think, because personally, I would not like him in my group if I was a woman. The next dubious issue is that every member of this group will be coming to his party. And, of course, the final and most alarming red flag, glowing brightly like the rotating beacon on a speeding ambulance, is his assurance that I'll be going home with one of them, thanks to his perfect wing-man charms. Has he learned nothing from the group? I suppose I'll go to the party, but the strongest draw is my curiosity to find out what the rest of the women think of his smarmy self.

Two days later, I return from lunch to discover an envelope on my desk. This is not a simple white envelope or even one of those pastel envelopes sold with greeting cards. And it's certainly not one with our company logo, which can be found in great quantity in the supply room. Instead, this envelope has a gorgeous curving pattern on the front, reminiscent of the gilt ormolu found on antique porcelain. I open it carefully so as not to tear this precious linen missive.

Inside the envelope, on heavy cream paper with raised lettering and a light floral scent, I find a party invitation. The person throwing this party is not identified, and there's no return address. But the party is on the same night as Mister Jerk's, and—the invitation states—is a surprise for him, so it must be kept secret. On the evening of the party, a clever ruse will bring Mister Jerk who will be delighted and amazed by all the love.

Now I'm not ready to shower Mister Jerk with love, but someone clearly is, and unlike his party, this one has a higher potential for greatness because it's being held at The Edge, the best performance venue in Palo Alto. How can I refuse?

For the next few weeks, the buzz at work is a subdued discussion of this secret party, which if I'm not wrong, includes all of us in the lab. Nobody can figure out why Mister Jerk is being honored on this day because it's not his birthday or anything else of significance. The mystery makes everyone curious, and they all agree to go to The Edge that night, both for a better party and also because Mister Jerk will be there too. His party is obviously off.

On the night of the party, there's excitement in the air as the whole lab gathers at The Edge. The place can hold hundreds of people, so it feels a little empty, even though there must be dozens of us in attendance with more arriving all the time. The music is loud, snacks and drinks are abundant, and people are having a blast. I even see a number of unfamiliar women who mingle well and turn out to be members of Mister Jerk's women's group. Those I talk to admit that when he insisted on joining the group, they felt bad refusing him. As I expect though, they are dubious about his so-called feminist side, and some of them think he's a giant buffoon. But one of the members of the group surprises me by claiming responsibility for tonight's party. I figure that if the people in Mister Jerk's women's group are honoring him with a party, they must not hate him too much.

The Dead Snails takes the stage. They like to make noise whenever they can, so tonight is a great excuse for another appearance. The lead singer starts by welcoming everyone, then he goes on and on about how jazzed they are to be playing at The Edge and how lucky we are to be able to party in this awesome music palace.

It makes me wonder if the band is also behind this party, perhaps in partnership with the women's group. It must have taken some serious coin to rent a space this big, especially on a Friday night, so a joint effort seems reasonable. Besides, The Dead Snails would love to say they'd played The Edge. Using Mister Jerk as an excuse could simply be a red herring, throwing us off the trail. And since nerds, even nerd bands, like puzzles, this one is perfect. I kick back as the band dives into their set, filling the room with gut-pounding rhythm. Out on the dance floor, everyone gyrates to the mix of catchy covers and fresh original tunes.

After dancing for a while, I escape outside to cool off, and who should be there but Wild Man Matt, a man who is stoned all day, every day, but still manages to program computers. He's passing around a fat joint, and after I take a hit, the party officially elevates to stratospheric levels.

Dakota Ronwood is out there too, stoned like the rest of us. Even as a young girl, people shortened her name to

Dacron, and nobody in the lab has ever called her anything else. Short and thin with a bob of blonde hair, her raspy voice speaks quickly to maximize the information flow. The two of us get into a deep discussion about our mysterious party hosts. I offer my theory that the band has partnered with the women's group, but Dacron shakes her head.

"I don't think the band's part of it. They just love any excuse to party."

I nod. "You could be right. One of the women from the group said she was responsible for this, but I still don't understand the connection to Mister Jerk. None of them has anything nice to say about the guy. Why would they throw a party for him?"

Dacron laughs at that. "Yeah, they like him and then, they don't. I heard they secretly shifted their weekly meeting time an hour earlier, so they have a chance to talk before he shows up."

"Aha, so you're saying they threw this party grudgingly, torn about their feelings."

Dacron shrugs at this, and our conversation continues like most stoned dialogues, winding randomly from parties to movies to the meaning of life. At some point, I find myself on the dance floor, then I'm back outside in the cool night air, this time with a beer. The party flows effortlessly.

As the night fades, the band finishes, and recorded music takes over. Some of my friends start to leave, making the rounds to say goodbye. Before Leap departs, he shakes his head and comments that we never saw Mister Jerk. Wasn't he supposed to be here for the event? Could he have missed it?

I wonder, too. I've been so busy enjoying myself that I never noticed any special activity. Perhaps it happened when I was outside getting high, but as I look around the venue, I have to admit that the guest of honor is nowhere to be seen. We puzzle over the omission but give it no further thought.

But on Monday, the lab is buzzing with the news. Mister Jerk was not there, and he didn't even know about the party. Instead, he spent all night at home, waiting for someone to arrive and growing more upset by the hour. In the end, nobody came, and now he's thoroughly infuriated. When he confronts me about this, I'm too embarrassed to mention the surprise party that was supposed to be in his honor, and I mumble some lie about being busy that night. Far be it for me to make his failed party into more of a loss.

At lunch, everyone engages in quiet conversation about the awesome party, the missing guest of honor, and most particularly, who threw the event. Some people think the band was responsible, but one of the band members is there, and he assures us they did not. That leaves the women's group as the prime culprit, but I still don't understand the lie about honoring Mister Jerk unless they did this to spite him. When he finally arrives at the table, people quickly revert to superfluous topics. As expected, he tosses a few barbs to those who promised to come over and didn't, but everyone deflects his words easily—something they've been learning to do for some time. After lunch, I return to my office without any clarification about what happened.

But later in the afternoon, I'm walking down the hall when I see AP moving briskly with a bundle of paper held close to her chest. She usually moves more casually, but right now, the energy she exudes is far from relaxed, so I turn to watch as she ducks into the printer room. She emerges quickly, now free of the clutched bundle, which ignites my curiosity. I make sure she's well down the hall and out of sight before I step into the room. Nothing seems out of order, and I can't spot a pile of paper that looks like what she was carrying, but as I'm about to leave, I see it in the recycling bin. AP has just dumped a fat pile of unused envelopes, all richly engraved with a very familiar curving pattern.

Art Direction

We're sitting in the lunchroom when Surf stomps over and holds his tray an inch above the table before letting it go, his mouth a tight grimace as the tray slams the remaining distance with a loud crash. The water cup on the tray sloshes, and he raises his fist, ready to spill the rest of it, then pauses for a few seconds and finally releases a noisy exhale, slumping down in his seat.

Everyone looks to him, unsure if he wants support or silence. Unafraid of any blowback from making the wrong decision, I break the ice. "What's eating you, Surf?" I can't resist a good story, and this promises to be interesting.

Surf cocks his head and gives me a level stare, then drawls, "Ah fuckin' hate Art Directors."

I nod and smile with comprehension. Surf is being worked over by the corporate media machine, which has latched onto his research and wants to use it for publicity. This is his own fault, unfortunately, for creating the first computer-generated picture with spectacular quality. He programmed an image of two spheres—one glass and the other mirrored—floating above a checkerboard. It's photo-perfect, showing every reflection, every bend of light, and every shadow. This is the first computer-generated picture that looks like a camera took it, and everyone in the lab has been marveling at it for weeks.

Uncle Pavel, our lab director, shared the image with his management, and before long, corporate PR came knocking. They want to use this in company reports, magazine ads, recruiting pamphlets, and more. It's a wonderful opportunity, but not without perils. And in this case, the peril consists of ignorant bureaucrats and media-grunts who think they know better.

Surf is a good-looking fellow from North Carolina with waves of dark hair and a winning smile that can go far in the promotion of this work. His name is Whitaker Turlock but he's called Surf because of his deep love of Surf music, with jangling guitar riffs and pounding beats. He plays this music often, and when he's deep in coding, the volume gets cranked higher to compensate for the fact that he's deaf in one ear. During these intense moments of programming, the music draws me to his office, and I watch his fingers fly; the clacking of keys drowned by the instrumentals of Dick Dale, The Chantays, and others. A mathematical superstar, he's pioneered several graphics ideas, as his latest stunning image shows.

After a few bites of lunch, Surf has calmed enough to explain further. "They don't like the colors on the checkerboard. Can ya believe that? Who gives two shakes of a rat's ass about somethin' like that?"

I squint at him. "So change the color." I don't see how this is such an ordeal. By tweaking one number in his program, the checkerboard color will change. I may not know all the math behind his work, but I've no doubt that coloring the checkerboard is easy.

"Well, sure." His mouth twists as his head slowly shakes. "But the program takes three hours to render, so I change it, then I gotta twiddle mah thumbs all day waitin' for a new picture. Can't get any work done while it's happenin' cause it sucks down everthin'. Wasted all mornin' on a new image, an' guess what? They still hate the color an' want me to change it again. Now the whole day is lost. I'm bein' art-directed to death."

I chuckle lightly. When Surf first created this picture, he gave a technical talk to explain how he did it, and everyone was amazed that he could produce it in only three hours. From what his program needed to do, I was surprised it didn't take days. It's massively complex, and although he asked for a new computer to help him do this, management balked. Now his machine is on overload trying to keep up. With nothing to do in the afternoon, Surf remains at the lunch table longer than the rest of us, and everyone offers ineffective words of support on their way back to work.

Fortunately, I hear "Pipeline" cranked loud the next day and wander past Surf's office to see him working away. He's clearly not waiting for his machine to spit out another picture, so I'm encouraged that he got beyond the art directors. But when I continue down the hall, I see the public-relations crew in a conference room with three versions of Surf's picture on the wall, each with a slightly different checkerboard color. They're gesturing at the wall and arguing, so I walk on quickly to avoid being sucked into their nonsense.

The next day, there are even more versions of the picture on the wall, and the differences are growing more and more subtle. I duck into Surf's office between songs and take a seat.

"You seem to be back at work, so I'm guessing they approved the final checkerboard color."

Surf rolls his eyes. "Not even close. Did two more yesterday an' one that ran overnight. They're still not happy."

"But you're working while you crank out the pictures. Did you borrow someone else's computer?"

Surf shrugs. "Somethin' like that. This better end soon if these people 'spect to live to an old age."

He's clearly not in the mood to talk, so I offer my sympathy and move on.

Two days later, the PR crew is gone, and Surf arrives merrily at the lunch table. "Had to redo that damn picture ten times before they approved it."

"Whoa, Surf. That must have wasted days of computer time. Did you find a way to speed it up because you seemed to be working through it all."

"Yep, found a great way to speed it up. Had three versions of the picture, and just cycled through them. Each time they asked for a new one, they'd get one of the three, goin' round and round. When they got the original picture the fourth time, they thought it was fabulous. Didn't even notice that they'd rejected it three times before. Far as they could tell, it was mah best work yet."

Hot Tub Justice

I'm at the yearly lab picnic with dozens of nerds, all eating, drinking, smoking, playing, and generally running around Foothill Park. After a decent lunch, I climb a shady hill to get away from everyone so I can relax and digest, but to my surprise, Standard is there, scanning the activity below. We sit in silence for a few minutes, but I can see him glance my way too often, practically bursting to say something, so I politely ask him what's on his mind. He laughs, then he turns toward me and gets comfortable. This could be good.

He starts with a long exhale. "You know that All lives with a bunch of people in an old mansion in Palo Alto."

All is a nerd from Stanford who works at another lab in Menlo Park. Her name is Alice Linda Lewis, but back at Stanford, they used initials for email addresses, so she became ALL. Unfortunately, the name "all" has a different meaning to some computers, and there were occasions when people wanted to send Alice a message but mistakenly sent it to everyone, which was troublesome. All doesn't have that confusing email address anymore, but the nickname has stuck. She's a good-looking woman with long dark wavy hair, an intense and direct personality, and at the moment, she's dating Standard, so there's got to be more to this story than her big old group-house.

Standard gets right to the point. "Well, the mansion happens to have a huge hot tub that's great for parties. And last night, All hosted one for her female nerd friends."

He cracks a small smile and shakes his head slowly, his amusement over a simple gathering of women in computing no doubt a harbinger of much more. Turning back to me, he begins by listing the party attendees: Dacron, AP, Blue, Charlie, and John—all women—including the two with men's nicknames.

"Sounds like fun, but I know you're going somewhere with this. Out with it."

Standard looks around to make sure there's nobody else nearby. Finally, he leans closer and lowers his voice. "Slick showed up. Someone must have mentioned the party at work, and he overheard."

Aha, that's rather unfortunate. Slick is a true lowlife who talks in an overly smooth way, like an old-time Vegas lounge host who tells nonstop sexist jokes. Even men cringe at his level of misogyny, so I can only imagine what would happen if he showed up at a women's hot tub party.

Horrified at the possibilities, I roll my eyes. "Did he strip down and try to get in the tub?"

Standard chuckles mildly. "No way. He was fully dressed, and he had a camera. He shouted out, 'Hey, girls!' Then he started snapping pictures, his flash doing rapid-fire damage."

I groan. "Oh, God. No." The guy's an embarrassment. I turn to scan the picnic area, but I don't see Slick.

"If you're looking for him, he's not here yet." Standard looks around too, then he turns back at me. "Let me finish this story because things are still happening. Anyway, after Slick takes the pictures, Dacron leaps out of the tub and chases him, stark naked."

Now this has positive potential. Some pushback. Especially coming from Dacron, who I can imagine could inflict serious damage. She's the biggest bundle of energy anyone knows, so the thought of her chasing Slick has me laughing. He doesn't stand a chance.

"Does she hunt him down and skin him alive?" I figure I'm allowed to dream.

"Better!" Standard smirks. "She's all, 'Say, that's a real fancy camera. Can I play with it?' And he sneers, 'Sorry but you'd never learn to operate this sophisticated equipment. It's too complicated for you.' Which is ridiculous since Dacron works with deep-space telemetry, and besides, she has a hobby as an auto mechanic. She even imported a French Citroen and installed air-shocks on it so she could raise and lower the car from the dashboard, making her the first nerd lowrider. At home, she's the fix-it person; her long-time boyfriend is a psychiatry graduate student and grateful to have Dacron to keep everything working. So, it's beyond absurd that she wouldn't know how to use Slick's camera."

Standard snorts with mild amusement. "She catches him pretty quickly and they struggle over the camera. Slick is too cocky and possibly distracted by a naked woman smashing her fists into his face and grabbing at the camera's neck strap. Before long, she's wrestled it away from him, and now he's chasing her, yelling 'That is an expensive camera, little girl!' So, she turns to him and says, 'I wonder how this works.' Then she pops open the back, pulls out the film, and tosses the camera on the ground."

"Yes." Standard and I fist bump for Dacron.

"Yes, indeed." Standard nods his agreement. "At about this point, All comes over with a towel for Dacron, and tries to get Slick to stop ruining the party. But Slick can't let it go.

He starts abusing Dacron, making jokes about her body, her looks, the usual sexist crap. He actually threatens to spank her for ruining his pictures, so she throws down the ultimate demand. She tells him that if he doesn't apologize and leave, he'll never drive his new car again, which she knows he loves dearly."

I'm impressed with that because it's a serious threat. If anyone can work a car, it's Dacron, so Slick should be worried. He bought a new BMW a few weeks ago, and he's been boasting about its fancy drive-by-wire feature that replaces many of the old-fashioned linkages with wires. Instead of hoses full of brake fluid running from the pedal to the wheels, there's a wire running to individual braking motors. Plenty of other functions are electrical instead of mechanical, making the car an early example of computer technology. And of course, Slick loves it because it makes him a trendsetter, once again proving that his nickname is apropos.

I give Standard a look. "Did he apologize? I'm guessing not. Did she take his car away?"

Standard looks at his watch then studies the people below. This time he sees Slick and points him out. "I figured it would take him a bit longer to get here today. He ended up losing a lot more than the car. See what he's doing?"

I turn to look down the hill and see Slick slowly working the crowd, moving from person to person quickly, sometimes staying to chat for an extra minute or two, never more. Everyone he sees gives him a gesture of sincerity, a handshake or a pat on the back. And that's when I figure it out. Slick is leaving the company. He's saying goodbye.

Slick notices the two of us up on the hill, and he starts our way.

Standard grins. "Watch this."

When Slick gets up to us, he greets us somberly and, as we already know, announces that he's quitting.

Standard acts sympathetic and asks, "What happened?"

Slick's lip quivers for a few seconds as he considers how to answer, then he suddenly grows angry and shouts, "She's your damned girlfriend, Standard, and her party ruined me."

Standard steps back. "You weren't invited, Slick. You owe them an apology."

Slick pauses, his face scrunching up even tighter. "So, you know about that curse on my car."

Standard sighs. "Yeah, I heard about that. How's it working out for you?"

Slick gives him a decidedly unfriendly scowl. "The car's fine. That stupid woman just let the air out of my tires, so her curse was a big bullshit bluff. It's the rest of my life that's crumbling. I got fired, and I'm also losing my wife. While I was getting dressed down by the boss, she called to tell me she's leaving. The car is the only thing I still have."

Standard rubs his chin. "So, you're saying that Dacron didn't ruin your car?"

"Nah. I called my mechanic, and he's bringing a flat-bed truck to haul it into the shop. It'll be back in no time, and the rest ... I'll live." Slick swallows hard and forces a grimace as he turns to walk off. "Later, losers."

After he's gone, I turn to Standard with huge eyes. "OK, explain. How did that happen?"

Standard shakes his head. "Let's get out of here. Picnic's nearly over, and I've got work to do. You can ride with me, and I'll tell you all about it." We wander to the parking area and get in his car.

As we're driving back, Standard explains. "You need to know that Dacron only wanted to take Slick's car. She never meant it to cost him his job or his wife. But at the hot tub party last night, the women were talking about Slick a half hour before he showed up. There wasn't a woman there who hadn't experienced the guy's abuse. So, when he did appear, they worried he'd overheard their gossip. They'd said some pretty nasty stuff about him, stories of him grabbing them from behind in the copy room or making rude comments during meetings."

"Sure." I grunt. "Everyone knows about Slick. He's pathetic. But what's that got to do with him losing his job and his wife?"

"Wait for it." Standard holds out a hand. "You see, AP told a story about how she was in a meeting with Slick once and watched him sign on to the lab systems with a password that was all one key that he hammered repeatedly. She watched him more closely the next time and discovered it was the number one, typed eight times. So, after he ruined the hot-tub party, a bunch of them logged into Slick's account just to let off steam. And when they did, they discovered some fairly damning items, including the fact that he's been using company money for himself, buying expensive appliances and fancy vacations. So one of them, All won't say who, sent an anonymous message to the lab director about it. That's how Slick got fired."

"And his wife?" I know Slick cheats on her. He's been seen at too many conferences with different women, and he disgustingly *boasts* that she doesn't know. He's a miserable excuse for a husband, and his wife will probably be better off without him. But why did she decide to leave him today?

Standard blows out a long breath. "Well, it's complicated, and it all happened so quickly that I'm still surprised. The lab director got the message about Slick's misuse of company funds this morning, so he started the exit process. HR froze his computer accounts, and Inkstain, the business manager, was given access to Slick's files so he could investigate more fully. But while he looked through the files, he found one called 'conquests' which has a list of every woman he's bedded, including dozens of them since he got married. So Inkstain sent the file to Slick's wife."

I like Inkstain, a guy who keeps a fistful of pens in his shirt pocket and still wears those shirts, even when leaking pens have left permanent black marks. But if he's going to reveal private information so carelessly, I'm not sure I should trust him with any secrets from now on. With a furrowed brow, I turn to Standard. "Why would Inkstain do that? His job is to find the embezzlement, not explore Slick's personal life."

"Yeah, but how do you think Slick got the job here? Inkstain is his brother-in-law; sending the file wasn't a random act of gossip, he was sending pertinent information to his sister."

I laugh at the coincidence. "Wow! Dacron wanted to destroy Slick's car but ended up destroying his job and his marriage instead."

"Oh, no, not *instead*." Standard shakes his head as we pull into the lab parking lot. "That car is toast, believe me. Slick just doesn't know it yet." He gets out of his car, and I follow him into the building, curious to learn about Slick's car, but all Standard will say is, "You'll see." Then he wanders off.

The first person I encounter when I reach the lab is Give Me All What We Have, a fellow researcher who, like Dacron, is a car enthusiast. He shows me a set of car keys. "Something's seriously wrong with Slick's car. I've never seen anything like it."

He leads me back outside to the parking lot. Along the way, he spots Dacron returning from the picnic, and he waves her over, knowing she'll be interested. The three of us gather around Slick's car, sitting much lower with its flat tires.

Give Me All What We Have holds up the key. "Slick gave me this so I could help load it when the flatbed arrives. I haven't played with one of these, so I got in and tried to start it, just for kicks. And take a look at this!"

When he opens the car door and pushes the start button on the dashboard, the entire console lights up red, half of it flashing menacingly. There's no engine sound, and the car is complaining about every possible error. This is the sad little car that can't.

Give Me All What We Have rubs his chin. "I've read about this model, with the drive-by-wire cleverness that runs an electrical backbone down the car." He works his mouth for a moment, then he wags a finger at the car. "If that backbone failed, it might look like this: a total collapse of the car's functions."

Dacron stares at the dashboard. "That sounds right to me."

"So what?" I timidly interject into this gathering of car-talk nerds. "If the cable is dead, put in a new one."

Dacron and Give Me All What We Have burst into laughter. She explains the unfortunate automotive truth. "First, it's a super-expensive part, but worse, to install it, you have to disassemble nearly the entire car, removing every panel and plenty of major components, too. Then you have to reconnect hundreds of wires. It's a huge and tricky job that costs almost as much as a new car."

"Plus ..." Give Me All What We Have frowns as he looks at the now-inert pile of shiny metal. "The car would never be the same after such a rebuild. If the cable fails, the car is totaled."

Now he turns to smile at Dacron. "Did you do something to this car?"

"Me?" She holds a hand to her chest. "All I did was let the air out of his tires. I certainly didn't crawl under the car and open an access panel." She shakes her head. "And I definitely didn't use a pair of heavy-duty cutters to slice the big round cable inside." Her eyes shine brightly. "I just kept my promise from last night. Slick will never drive this car again."

Stinking Badges

As I come into work, two guards have surrounded Fash and are escorting him out the door. Fash is no troublemaker, but these guards scowl and spread their arms threateningly as if eager to attack at the slightest provocation. He sees me and turns to say something, but they hustle him away with a warning to have a proper badge when he returns.

I'm concerned, so I follow him out to the parking lot. As usual, Fash opens with a comment about my attire. "Looking good today. Socks actually match your shirt."

I look at myself, and I guess it's so, though not as a result of any forethought on my part. But Fash, whose name is Lorenzo Peters, cares about clothing color enough to have earned his nickname. He's the lab's fashion expert, a big and muscular man with wavy dirty blond hair. He's also an expert on computer graphics, and his fashion sensibilities show up colorfully in the animated videos he makes. The rest of us nerd boys have no color sense at all.

I wave away his compliment and ask why he's been thrown out of the building. I might as well be asking for the weather report from Tierra del Fuego, because he ignores me and continues with his fashion advice.

"Nobody in the lab cares about their appearance, which is sad, you know. Look at me today. Rust socks and a cinnamon-colored shirt. And my belt is sangria for the perfect contrast. See how they match?" I doubt if I could name any of those colors, let alone tell them apart; and I fail to see how they match, other than the fact that they're all brown. But it doesn't matter because I'm used to this. Fash's sense of style always falls on deaf ears in the lab.

The most recent news about Fash is that he's gay. Now any normal person with even the slightest amount of "gaydar" would know this and fail to be surprised. But interestingly, none of the nerd boys in our lab had figured it out. He was married, after all, and to a woman, so we assumed he was merely fashion-conscious. But two months ago, he announced his marriage was a sham and he was coming out. Half the guys in the lab went home to tell their wives this surprising news, only to be rewarded with eye rolls from these patient women who'd known Fash was gay all along.

I still don't understand why he got thrown out of the building, so I try a different approach. "Are you quitting, Fash?"

"Are you kidding? I just got new business cards. Check this out." He reaches into his wallet and hands me a card. Most of us want to have an important-sounding title on our cards so we can impress friends, colleagues, and family. Not Fash. He found a loophole in the company's business-card rules that allows any job title to be printed. His card proudly announces, "Lorenzo Peters, Animated Character."

I laugh, then I tell him about Leap's business cards. This guy likes to take other people's cards and turn them into his own. Last week, he showed everyone his latest card, which was originally from a towing company, a little cartoon tow truck in the corner. But where it once said Jackson Towing, he had drawn a line through the words and written our company's name. Where the tow-truck operator's name was printed, he'd struck it out and written his own. Everything on the card was altered meticulously, the only unchanged part being the location, Palo Alto, California. He intentionally avoids blacking out the old information, using thin lines to make it abundantly obvious this was once someone else's card. Leap spends serious time on these cards, so he has only a few, and although he likes to show them, he rarely gives them away.

Fash appreciates Leap's approach to business cards, then he gets in his car to go home. I stop him before he can start the car. "Come on, Fash. Dish about the badge."

He blows out a breath and gestures to the passenger seat, promising to return to work when he's fixed this problem. I get in, and we drive off.

After a few blocks, Fash turns to me. "Do you know about Big Andy's theory of computer research? He says 'research is like Grand Theft Auto: you get three to five.' And he's right. After that many years, research labs sour and everyone runs like termites from a burning log. I've been in three labs already, and this one's doing fine, but not for long. Research is only done at successful companies that have some spare coin to spend on stuff that won't turn a quick profit. As long as there's money in the bank, a research lab seems like a good idea. But when times get tough, the labs are the first to go."

I agree that computer researchers live with uncertainty, but since there's always some other company doing well, we bounce back easily.

Fash agrees with that, too, then he points to his glove box. "Look in the blue envelope."

Inside are three company badges, all with his picture from places he's worked. I turn to him with big eyes, waiting for an explanation about how he managed to keep these, because badges must be surrendered when you leave a company.

"I collect them. It's easy enough. When I know I'm quitting, I show up at work one day without my badge and tell them I lost it. They always replace it happily, and then I've got an extra one for my collection. Notice how my old SunTex badge looks a lot like our current ones? When I interviewed here, I flashed it and walked right in the door. Nobody noticed, and I showed up for my job interview by sitting down in Uncle Pavel's office."

I chuckle. "Bet he didn't like that."

"You're right. He took me back to the guard desk and made me sign in properly. Still, badges are good to have."

"Except when the guards bust you for having the wrong one. Is that what just happened?"

"Eh, not quite. See, I got this idea that my badge should match my outfit, so I 'lost' my badge a few times. I wore a different color shirt each time so when they retook my picture, I'd be sporting a different color. Got six badges now, each with me wearing a different shirt, so now I can accessorize my outfits properly. Unfortunately, as I came into the building today, I was stupidly boasting to a friend that my outfit matched my badge, and the guard, who'd heard my lost-badge complaint too often, figured it out."

Getting Grape

As I approach Standard's office, I hear a deep laugh that continues so long, he's still chuckling when I get to the door. He's on the phone and manages to control himself enough to finish the conversation.

"Oh, that's amazing. You are *too* much." He listens a bit, then ends with, "Yes, dinner at the new Mexican place. See you at seven."

This must be All, the nerd woman he's dating. She's obviously done something clever, so I drop in before Standard can resume coding.

"What happened?"

He's still smiling from the news. "All got Grape real good. I can hardly believe it." A few aftershock chortles bubble to the surface.

Grape is an old friend of All's, both former Stanford students now working in the valley. His name is Martin Slalom, an average-size man with a big bushy beard and curly but balding brown hair. Everyone calls him Grape because of his total dedication to wine. You can't dine out with him unless the restaurant has the finest selections, which he tastes with authority then explains in abundant detail.

I'm curious to know how All got him so I inquire, hoping he's not too badly affected, but Standard switches topics. "Do you know about the bag of sesame sticks?"

I wonder how Grape, who is an epicure, would have anything to do with a bag of greasy munchies, so I shake my head and gesture for an explanation.

"It started a few years ago. All and I went over to Grape's place for dinner, and we brought a sandwich bag full of sesame sticks. You've got to bring something when you visit friends, and All thought they might do. Grape just set them aside, and the bag wasn't mentioned again. Then, a few days later, Grape was at her place, and he brought the bag as *his* gift, which we all agreed was pretty funny. So, it became a meme. Whenever we got together, which we do often, the last one to have the sesame sticks would bring it as a fake gift, making it a token that balanced whose turn it is to host."

I'm amused but curious. "Always the same bag, or did you buy new ones now and then?"

"The same bag, and the plastic soon grew cloudy from constant handling and oily contents. At one point, All felt bad that we were bringing this ugly bag of inedible food, so she got show tickets to see Jonathan Richman and slipped a ticket in the bag. When Grape came by the next time, the sandwich bag was taped to a bottle of wine. The sesame sticks, already symbolic, had become a greeting card that we attached to gifts.

"Then one day, Grape came over and the sticks were growing blue fuzz. It was gross, and we realized the game had to end. The joke had run its course, so we had a memorial service for the good-old days as we tossed it in the trash."

I nod at the story's conclusion. "Those snacks are full of preservatives. I'm surprised the joke went on long enough for them to rot."

Standard shrugs. "We kept opening the bag to put smaller gifts inside, so perhaps that shortened their lifespan. And the joke did go on for years, as do plenty of others that we keep telling past their sell-by date. Look at the way Grape names his pets Eric to honor the *Monty Python* skit where someone gives that name to his dog, his cat, and his fish. Grape got a fish named Eric, then a turtle named Eric, then another fish named Eric because the first one died, and so on. I think he's up to his fourth fish, and they're all named Eric. He wants a bird now, and you can guess what he'll name it."

I chuckle at this one. "It's all jokes with Grape."

"Almost." Standard shakes his head. "He takes his wine seriously; I'll tell you that. Invested in a Napa winery recently and claims to have a few cases handy for all possible futures. Grape loves his grapes."

None of this explains the outburst of humor minutes ago. "So, what's going on with All and Grape?"

"Oh, yeah. That's All, the matchmaker. She's got this amazing knack of understanding people, and she's able to get them both jobs and partners. The jobs skill is less surprising because she's super connected here in the valley —knows who's hiring and what they want. When she meets someone new to the area, she can recommend a place they might like, and she's arranged at least three or four jobs."

"Did she get Grape a job?"

"She's been trying for some time, and he could certainly use one—he's languishing and hates his current project. All has suggested a few places, but he always ends up rejecting the move. The guy is content to be stuck."

I figure it's the other kind of matchmaking Standard's talking about. "OK, did All match him with a woman?"

"She's been trying on that front, too. But Grape's pretty resistant. He's got a list of requirements that are hard to meet. Must be a certain height, certain weight, certain hair color. Must be interested in specific subjects like sailing, humor, music, and wine. All came close last year, but the date failed because the woman didn't share his appreciation of punk rock. Grape's ridiculous that way.

"Then three weeks ago, All was wondering if Grape would like a new friend of hers from work. But she has red hair, and I know that's off Grape's list, so I warned All that the two of them wouldn't make it past a first date. Still, All thought it would be nearly perfect, and she insisted that they had to meet. For the next few days, we discussed this match, which I saw as a match made in hell. Of course, All was undeterred and planned all sorts of ways to get them together. And guess what? She did it. She was just telling me that Grape called. They've reached the critical two-week mark, and they're both surprisingly happy. It's not wedding bells, but it's another notch in All's matchmaking belt."

"Nice," I concede. "But what had you laughing so hard?"

Standard smiles. "It's how she made Grape stop long enough to give the woman a chance. All setup a blind date for them, then filled a sandwich bag with sesame sticks and gave it to her to bring along. It broke the ice perfectly."

The Secret Question

Our lab is growing quickly, and candidates show up for jobs every few days. It's a good sign because the company is committed to computer research and has devoted resources, office space, and most important, money. The only downside is the time it takes to interview these people and make a decision. It's not a simple process.

Our lab pours over resumes at weekly hiring meetings and chooses the ones who will make the first cut. This stage is easy because some job seekers stand out and others have uninspired resumes. Occasionally someone has strong feelings about an otherwise poor applicant, and we generally let the candidate through out of respect for their advocate and to avoid extended and possibly heated discussions. We also let them through because it's not that difficult to do.

Once job seekers pass the resume process, the lab digs a little deeper by contacting their references. The computing field is small enough these days that many of the people who write a letter of recommendation are familiar to someone in our lab, as a former coworker or simply an acquaintance from a conference. One of us is tasked with a frank conversation with the reference-writer about the candidate's potential.

After we complete the reference check, the job seeker's resume returns to the next hiring meeting where we consider the final test: should we bring them here for an in-person interview. Video conferencing doesn't exist yet, and nothing is as good as a deep technical chat, so they have to come to our lab and meet everyone face-to-face. This can be costly if the candidate is out of town and we have to fly them, house them, and feed them, so the lab is careful about the people they invite.

And that's when the huge time cost rears its ticking head because candidates can expect to spend all day in our lab, talking with many of us, which results in far less work getting done. But it's worthwhile because if they pass, an offer is extended, and we hopefully have a new coworker.

Of course, even the job offer is tricky because there are other labs in the valley, and good candidates have multiple choices. We have to make our best offer if we want them here. Nothing is more frustrating than losing a candidate who we've spent hours courting, just because our offer wasn't competitive.

On the day of an interview, one of us is assigned the task of hosting the candidate: meeting, greeting, and moving them around. The day is scheduled carefully so all the interested parties get a chance to meet the person. At some point, usually early on, the candidate gives a presentation to the entire lab. It's typically just a repeat of work they've described many times before, but their ability to give a coherent talk is under review here as is their ability to answer hard questions. If they underwhelm, they won't get a job.

Another key moment in the interview day is lunch, where we all dine together. Here, each of us can get to know this person and see if there's an easy connection. After all, these people are going to be our colleagues, and if they're abrasive or tedious, we'll all be sorry.

But the heart of the interview is the individual meetings, where the candidate sits with us one at a time to learn what we do. It's a deep test of their potential. Do they understand our research? Do they have any new ideas about it? Could they really work with us? It's the individual interviews that determine a candidate's chance of getting a job.

* * *

I'm still at the table after a hiring meeting has ended, considering eight new resumes that just arrived. I scan them quickly and pull out two that seem promising. Red-Ink Vlad, the senior member of the lab, pushes his pile to the side and grins at me.

"What's your secret question?"

I raise an eyebrow. "Secret question?"

"You know. When the candidate is in your office for a one-on-one interview, what's the key question you ask that makes or breaks them? We all ask questions, but there's usually one that pushes the candidate above or below the bar for employment."

Now this is interesting because I do have such a question. My research in a small corner of computing hinges on a disputed assumption, so I ask their opinion of that assumption. If they're ignorant of it or disagree completely with my view, I quickly lose interest.

"Boring." Red-Ink Vlad smirks, slowly shaking his head. "Are you telling me your secret question is purely technical? Come on. You can do better than that."

"OK, Vlad. What's your secret question?"

"I ask them if they work on their own car. It has nothing to do with computers, but it shows whether or not they're tinkerers. Anyone who works on their car, even if they just change the oil occasionally, is someone willing to dive into a problem. But if they reject that task and let a mechanic handle it, I don't think they'll be a good fit here."

Mild is at the table, a smart but tediously boring fellow who deserves his nickname, and he begins a slow description of his secret question. "Brain teaser." It took him twice as long to say those two words as anyone else would have taken, so we collectively cringe as he continues his explanation. "You have twelve coins that weigh the same, except for one." Most of us know this puzzle, so we trade discrete eye rolls as he lays it out again. "You have a balance scale that tells if two piles weigh the same."

Oh lord, please make Mild finish this soon.

"You have to find the odd coin in just three weighings on the scale."

Oh good, he's done. But since he has our attention, he goes for the jugular.

"Some candidates—"

"Yeah, yeah, yeah," Endian cuts him off because most of us are in our twenties, with a mere half-century of life-expectancy left, so we've better things to do than listen to this fellow drone. Besides, some of us interviewed here after Mild was hired, so we already had to endure his brain teaser.

Endian has his own secret question. "I ask them if they're quick-and-dirty programmers—getting their code down sooner but messily—or if they're slow-and-methodical—taking extra time to study the task so they get it clean the first time. If they pick either one, I reject them. But if they rework my question, they pass. They might boast that they're quick *and* methodical, or they might tell me they start off quick, then return later to apply more methodical considerations once the program's been written. These are the people I want to hire."

Dacron, our radio expert, has her own secret question that involves circuit design. She makes them draw the schematic for a simple binary operation. If they know it cold, they're in. If they have to work it out, she can watch their thought processes and approve them. But if they claim any inability in the task, they're rejected.

Give Me All What We Have, a man with a longer nickname than one should have, surprises us with his secret: lunch. As far as he's concerned, it's all about the personality and much less about the technical know-how, which he leaves to others in the lab to decide. So, he sits near the candidate at lunch and asks about their life, their interests, their past, and their expected future. If they're personable, he approves them. But if they're tedious nerds with nothing else going on, it's a reject. I have to wonder where he was when Mild got the job.

Red-Ink Vlad then leans closer to us and lowers his voice. "Want to know what Uncle Pavel uses? As lab director, he talks to every candidate, so all of us met with him before being hired, and all of us answered his secret question correctly. He asks whether you like *Star Trek* or *Star Wars*." Vlad leans back to address everyone at the table. "What was your answer?"

I tell him I like *Star Trek*. Dacron and Give Me All What We Have agree. But Mild and Vlad claim to prefer *Star Wars*. Mild even has a Yoda bobblehead on his desk, still in the original packaging, so we know which side he chooses. The discussion devolves into a heated conversation where the two teams grow passionate about their answers, insisting they got jobs because they answered correctly. But Vlad knows better.

"You got your jobs because you picked one. Doesn't matter to Uncle Pavel which answer you give as long as you have a ready answer and are prepared to defend it. If you tell him that you don't care, have no interest in science fiction, or otherwise try to waffle, you don't get a job here."

Courtship

When QZP enters the lunch room, conversation quiets, and everyone turns to stare. There are three problems here, the least of which are the cuts on his face and ear, which make him look like he fought a feral beast and lost. Next in surprise would be the fact that he's holding hands with Drive-R, a graphic designer who I know he's been dreaming about. She's kept her distance since starting work at the lab, insisting she's not interested in nerds, but given the smile she's giving QZP, I'd say her feelings have changed. I'm happy for them.

Drive-R's real name is Sandra Driver, but everyone says her last name pirate-style, with an emphasis on the second syllable so it comes out, "Drive Arrrrr." With blunt bangs on shoulder-length brunette hair, she delivers rapid conversation and serious questions, something the nerds in the lab appreciate. Her job as a graphic designer is to add extra sparkle to polish our work, whether it be figures in papers, slides for talks, poster boards at big shows, or mockups of proposed gadgets. She's artistic relief to a group of people who aren't sure which end of a pencil to use.

QZP is a long-standing friend from school—thin and energetic with messy blonde hair that makes him look like a surfer dude. He loves outrageous gestures, especially those of a sexual nature. His idea of humor is to sneak up to people—both men and women—and hump their leg like a dog. He's there every Saturday night for the midnight *Rocky*

Horror Picture Show, always cross-dressed as the movie's hero, Frank-N-Furter. And once, when required to wear a shirt and shoes at a place of business, he wore a see-through mesh shirt and the skimpiest thong to cover his junk. Then, to further annoy the shopkeeper, he glued leather soles to the bottoms of his feet so he would indeed be shod even though it didn't appear that way.

When at work, QZP dresses normally, wearing standard nerd attire of jeans and a T-shirt. But one night at a party of lab people, the subject of underwear came up and the men were asked their preference of briefs or boxers. This was sufficient choice for most of us, but not QZP who boldly proclaimed that he wears women's underwear. He's not gay, as many of his former lovers can attest, and he's not really a transvestite. He just likes to act out as outrageously as possible.

Another side to QZP's strangeness is his moniker, which may stand for something, but nobody knows for sure what it is. His real name is Quincy Smith, so the acronym shares only one of the letters in his name. When asked about the Z and the P, he tells a long story about motorcycle racing, which doesn't fully answer the question, but at least it's entertaining. And there are quite a few motorcycle enthusiasts in the lab, so once they begin to talk about engines, handlebars, and helmets, they forget their curiosity about the letters Q, Z, and P.

It may be strange to see QZP's face cut up, and it may be stranger to see him snuggling with Drive-R, but the strangest change today is his hair. Gone is the surfer mane along with most of the hair on his head. He's not bald, but close, with a quarter-inch buzz-cut that makes him look somewhat military and causes the most alarm.

QZP and Drive-R sit down and share a sweet smile. The rest of us clamor for an explanation, so he raises his hand to quiet the room, then squanders the attention by unwrapping his sandwich and taking a bite. We abuse him roundly for that, so he laughs, then he tells us what happened.

"I was talking to Big Andy last week, telling him how much I admire Drive-R and how I've been trying to catch her eye for months. He suggested that since she's a visual artist, I had to do something visual to get her attention. As soon as he said this, I knew immediately what I was going to do."

Big Andy is known around the lab for his big talk, especially when it comes to science, sports, and women. He may well be an authority on the first two, but his understanding of women sometimes seems dubious, particularly to the women in the lab. However, since QZP has indeed managed to win Drive-R's heart, Big Andy might know a bit in this area, so everyone turns to look at him with a mix of curiosity and newfound respect. He gives a modest smirk and sits back to let QZP tell the tale.

"So here's the plan." QZP reduces it to a sound bite. "I installed my head in a computer rack." All around the table, eyes squint, heads tilt, and chins get scratched.

We've got plenty of computer racks. At the heart of our research lab, there's a big room filled with at least a dozen of them. Racks like these are about six feet tall and two feet wide, filled with pieces of equipment stacked all the way up. Screws on the sides of each piece hold it securely in place. Most of the racks are full, but as we get new machines and decommission the old ones, the racks start to look spotty. Sometimes there are gaping holes, just waiting for devices to be installed. QZP's plan is to stick his head out of one of those gaps.

The idea of QZP's smiling face in the middle of this broad expanse of hardware already has quite a few of us amused, and clearly the visual gag has been successful because Drive-R is laughing along with everyone else, but he advises us that this story is just getting started, so we settle in for more.

"One of the racks has a six-inch gap." QZP holds his hands against the sides of his head to show that he's measured it and knows he will fit. "Now, some of the equipment is fairly deep, which makes it impossible to get my head even close to the opening when coming from the back. The good news is the six-inch gap I chose has something deep below it but a fairly shallow piece of hardware above it, so I could lay on the lower box and slide my head right up to the opening. Unfortunately, I didn't consider the added room needed by my ears, and I didn't realize these racks have all sorts of screws and other connectors that can be sharp, making it difficult to get my head through."

This explains the cuts on his face and ears. Everyone gives QZP another round of laughter for that.

He rubs his bandaged ear. "I cut myself first thing, just as my head was half-way through the opening. It was tighter than I expected, and the equipment below me has a large, jagged edge. I considered pulling out and abandoning this plan, but I'd come this far and was already bleeding. Besides, Big Andy was waiting out front to help me, so I pushed on, figuring it would be just as painful to pull back at this point."

Big Andy interrupts the story to describe how ragged QZP's head looked by the time he'd poked it out of the rack.

When it first emerged, his hair was flattened against his head and had to be pulled away to give that look we've all come to identify with the hippie nerd. Big Andy took a few pictures, then he went to invite Drive-R into the machine room so she could appreciate the gesture.

At this point, Drive-R mentions how amused and touched she was to see QZP in this ridiculous pose. Sitting there in the machine room, they chatted for a while, and she even dabbed his bleeding ear. But when the joke had run its course, QZP found that he couldn't get his head back out. Apparently, it was a tight enough fit that it worked OK on the way in, but his ears were already in pain and kept getting caught by the hard metal edges on the way out. After a few attempts, he lost his desire to endure the passage again. QZP was stuck.

He and Big Andy discussed the problem, and they decided that some of the hardware above or below needed to be moved. These devices are only held in place with a few screws on the side, so Big Andy went in search of a screwdriver.

They soon discovered that the larger unit below QZP was not going to budge. First, it's held in with nearly a dozen screws, and second, it provides power to so many other pieces of equipment that it can't be disconnected without taking down half of the machines in the room. Instead, they agreed that the piece above QZP would be the one to pull, being only four inches high.

As Big Andy was about to do this, Drive-R examined the box above QZP and asked what it meant by the label, "terminal concentrator." This question caused the nerd boys to groan because terminal concentrators are simple machines, but they're heavily connected throughout the lab and can't be unplugged easily. The normal protocol for doing maintenance on a terminal concentrator is to announce the device will be going down, then give the users, who can be anywhere in the lab, five minutes to finish their work and get off. So Big Andy sent the shutdown message, then he came back to wait, while he and Drive-R teased QZP about his predicament.

After five minutes, Big Andy turned off the terminal concentrator and tried to unplug the various cables in the back, but there were too many of them, and he was afraid he wouldn't reconnect them properly, so he decided to pull it out of the rack while still connected. Unfortunately, to do this, he needed to rearrange several wires, untangling them so they'd be long enough to stretch when the unit was pulled forward. This operation took another five minutes, beginning to strain QZP's patience.

Finally, Big Andy came around to the front of the rack and unscrewed the terminal concentrator. This seemingly simple and relatively small unit was quickly detached, but nobody had considered it would now drop down onto QZP, nor did they realize it might be small, but it weighs forty pounds. Big Andy couldn't pull it all the way out since the wires were still connected in back, and he couldn't push it back through the rack since the mounting hardware was in the way, so the box laid on top of QZP, causing additional discomfort.

After a short discussion in which QZP rapidly shot down every alternative in favor of a solution that would free him sooner, they decided to unplug all the wires in the back so the unit could be fully removed. Of course, this also took time because Big Andy had to mark every wire and write them down so he could reconnect them properly. As an aside at this point, QZP tells us that if it were not for the sympathetic ministrations of Drive-R, this would be the worst day he'd experienced in a very long time, perhaps ever.

It turns out that Drive-R is the one who saved QZP. While Big Andy was in back, taking note of each wire, she noticed that the terminal concentrator has an unusual shape. It is four inches high in the rack, but only the front control panel is that tall. Behind the panel is a box only three inches high with a gap on top. This meant that the unit could be pulled out slightly, then lifted an inch, enough to let QZP escape. When she pointed this out, Big Andy ran around to the front of the rack to free his colleague.

Everyone at the lunch table is sore amazed by this tale of awkward playfulness, but there is one change QZP hasn't explained. Why did he cut his hair? He's explained how his head got bashed up, and how he and Drive-R have bonded over this experience. But why the haircut?

QZP explains that as he pulled his head from under the terminal concentrator, his long hair got sucked into the cooling fan of the power supply below him. Suddenly, he was stuck again and shouting in pain. Big Andy dropped the concentrator, afraid he was the cause of this discomfort, which of course made QZP yell even louder. It was Drive-R who saved the day by running to her office and returning with scissors, which she used to cut QZP's hair and free him. When he finally emerged, his hair had been hacked so badly that he realized he needed to cut it all off.

Dress Code

History tells us a king's reign often ends sooner than expected when they get murdered by their successors. Royalty is an unstable job, and the same can be said for corporate executives, who appear and then disappear before the ink on their business cards has dried. I never worry about a deposed executive because I know these people will do well, probably finding another position within hours, and also because I find such people to be a lower form of life than planaria. It's clearly not a job that holds much appeal.

The CEO of our company left a few weeks ago, and a new one has been hired. This particular executive comes from a household cleaning company, so his understanding of computers is limited. When he first arrives on campus and sees the strangely garbed nerds with sandals, tattered clothes, and rude T-shirts, he asks whether this is a Casual Friday event and is shocked to learn his new employees dress this way all the time. And that is why, now that management has settled in, they deliver a dress code memo.

Employees must be presentable, according to our new leader, because the reputation of the company demands it. I don't know what reputation he thinks is in jeopardy because the company is doing just fine. Instead, I suspect he's protecting his own reputation, which would be sorely damaged if his C-suite golf buddies found out about his slovenly workers.

Everyone in the lab wants to explain the Silicon Valley way to this new CEO, where casual is not only allowed, it's expected and sometimes even demanded. At lunch, I grouse about the stupidity of it all.

Acre, who worked at a small startup company for a while, tells the story of a major investor who came to visit one day. Acre asked his boss if he should dress up to impress the visitor, but the boss laughed at the offer and insisted that Acre dress as casually as ever or even more so. The boss understood that his tech people need to look the part. A nerd in a three-piece suit is as wrong as a fly with a bow tie; it's out of place, and nerds are so unaccustomed to such clothing they never wear it right. It sends the wrong message to investors.

Over the next few weeks, the dress code is the subject of entirely too much discussion. Guards at the building entrances are given discretion when admitting employees, and a few incidents are reported in which people are sent home instead of being allowed to work. It's an amusing situation, but it gets real one day when Big Andy is turned away because he's wearing shorts. He returns wearing pants, angry and primed for action.

Plenty of others in the lab agree with Big Andy. QZP, who entertains us with tales of his clothing misadventures, wants to come to work naked so he can make the boldest of statements. Mr. Rogers wonders where the dividing line is between shorts and pants. He still has pants from his prepubescent days when he was significantly shorter, and he promises to wear a pair tomorrow to test just how much of his calves can be visible before he's deemed to be wearing shorts. Everyone is puzzled by these new requirements.

Red-Ink Vlad, one of the older scientists in our lab, agrees fully with the dress code memo. He teases all the younger kids, which means everyone else, and reminds us there was once a time when appearance mattered. And yet, when I look at him more closely, I see clothes that have been used so much they're severely frayed, occasionally torn, and have entire patches thin enough to expose underwear or worse. His outfits may be formal and able to pass the new CEO's demands, but they're actually *less* worthy than the outfits worn by others in the lab.

A few workers from a different corporate division stage a protest, adorned more poorly than ever in an attempt to poke management into a more sensible attitude. Outrageously shabby men stand in the parking lot holding signs that demand freedom of dress. One or two women join, but they're not nearly as badly attired and are merely showing support.

Management responds by calling the police. Since these under-dressed workers aren't permitted in the building, when the police demand that they move on, they have to go home. It's an ugly scene, which nobody wants to repeat for fear that management will be more vicious next time.

Posters appear in the hallways to explain the new dress code. Each sign shows someone attired badly, with arrows and notes explaining why the clothes are inappropriate for a well-turned worker. It feels like a lecture from parents, and people respond appropriately with lots of yelling, swearing, and storming to rooms. But beyond that and some graffiti on the posters, the rebellion stalls out.

Then, a few days later, I hear laughter from down the hall, and I see that Big Andy has a sizable crowd in his office. They're packed tightly, speaking loudly, and laughing more frequently than any technical discussion merits. Apparently, he has a plan to defeat the onerous dress code, and everyone leaves his office with renewed enthusiasm for a quick solution.

I don't know much more about this, but the next afternoon, an announcement is made that the dress code has been rescinded. Either Big Andy nailed it precisely, or management caved by coincidence. At lunch, he explains what happened.

"I found the perfect way forward. QZP, Mr. Rogers, myself, and a few others went over to the executive wing and gathered outside the CEO's office. He invited us in, and we explained how his dress code was costing the company in poor morale, wasted employee time, overpriced posters, and extra guards. We assured him that if this doesn't stop, we'd find work elsewhere, and that would cost him even more. He caved instantly because he may not know computers, but he does know money."

Then Big Andy shows us a picture of them with the CEO. They're all wearing women's dresses, courtesy of their female nerd friends. These are decent, modest dresses that are perfectly acceptable under the company's dress code, which makes no mention of cross-dressing.

Car On Fire

"Hey, y'all! Check it out, there's a burning car out there." Surf is racing down the hall to tell everyone. He stops at my office, so excited that he shakes his hands like castanets. "Best view is mah office." He does a dance of joy, then continues his Paul Revere ride.

Burning cars may be common occurrences for action film characters, but it's not something I see in person very often. Never actually. And that seems to be the most common reaction around here. Everyone quickly gathers in Surf's office. He definitely has the best view.

One flight down and right across the street, a car is burning by the side of the road. Traffic moves past it, but no one has stopped to look. In fact, there are no people around at all. Just a lonely car, quietly simmering while the rest of the world drives by. And not far away, safe in our office building, I have a ringside seat.

The car is very polite about its immolation. No explosions, no twisted metal, not a single shooting jet of flame, this considerate car is keeping it mostly on the inside with licks of fire along the edges of the hood, making it look like a giant burner element that could roast a whole cow. But soon the engine compartment goes dormant, and the fire marches down the car. The dashboard ignites, with more colorful flames thanks to the electronics and plastics. Then the fire spreads through the interior, where soft carpets, plush seats, and velvet ceiling liners that once gave the comfort of home are now prime kindling. The ever considerate vehicle finishes its consumption with a relatively quick burn through the trunk, then it's done, leaving the car so thoroughly stripped that it doesn't even have paint anymore, just blackened metal.

When the fire was still at the front of the car, Surf's office was standing-room only, packed three deep at the window. But after a few minutes, everyone had their fill of this modern Yule log, and they'd traded enough burning car jokes, so their only option was to go back to work. By the time the trunk's meager supply of combustible materials gives it up, there are just three people left in the office: me, Surf, and Dacron. Surf and Dacron are two of the lab's automotive experts, and they've been discussing the technicalities of a burning car since the start.

The show is over, so I'm about to leave when Surf smiles at me and gives Dacron a nod. "Nice one."

Wait a minute. Nice one? This was Dacron's prank? Did she stage this automotive bonfire? Surf knows. No wonder he ran around the building calling everyone over. It also explains why his office had the best view. This is an inside job by the lab's car authorities, and I need to know more, so I stop Dacron from leaving and sit her back down, demanding that she and Surf tell me why that car burned.

Dacron raises both hands in a sign of surrender. "It was Alil's doing. Started at that party she threw. She and N have been doing the horizontal mambo for a few months, but they got into a tiff at the party over the rules of some stupid card game. Each of them declared themselves the winner according to their view of life, and insisted that any other interpretation would be pure ignorance. Feelings were sore all around."

Surf and I agree that Alil and N have been less tender toward each other at work.

"So Alil went into N's office earlier today and insisted that she was the absolute ruler of heaven, earth, and game rules. The great goddess, able to vanquish any enemy, yadda yadda. She warned him that anyone who disagreed would be truly sorry, and she formed her hand into a gun and pointed threateningly at him, warning that she'd shoot if he didn't concede. Then, out of courtesy to his meager mortal self, she pointed out the window and gave a warning shot to the car across the street. That car happened to be an old clunker I found in the junkyard. Surf and I had it wired with incendiary devices, and when we saw her aim at it, we lit it up." Dacron brightens considerably. "Wish we'd had some marshmallows."

Big-Time Music

We arrive at work to tragic news: Wings has died. Our lives will forever be diminished by the loss of our clever Czechoslovakian colleague. At least he died living up to his nickname. During a four-hour hang-gliding endurance run, he passed out and sailed into the side of a mountain. I stumble through the halls in a daze, too numb to focus on a computer but too immobilized to go home and deal with this privately. Wings will be missed.

A few days later, I see Standard, Iggy, and Boom, the remaining members of The Dead Snails. Wings was their drummer, so they've lost more than a work colleague. I offer my condolences and avoid making a comment about the irony of the band's name.

Iggy is sad, but he shrugs off the loss to the band. "We were falling apart anyway. Everyone in the lab wanted a piece of the action and kept showing up at band rehearsals. We had keyboard players, backup singers, even someone with an accordion, and we didn't have the heart to send them away. So honestly, losing Wings is tragic, but it's the perfect excuse to kill the band. Now we don't have to hurt anyone's feelings by telling them their musical contributions suck."

Boom and Standard agree with this, but they're hooked on playing music and admit to looking for other bands in the valley. Iggy isn't looking for another band, but he plans to give guitar lessons to AP, and he's sweet on her, so we know his musical plans have merit.

Two months later, Standard comes to my office with a pronounced bounce to his step. He waltzes over to a chair and drapes himself in it sideways, limbs helicoptering with enough energy to power ocean waves.

"I found a new band! There was a systems conference down in Monterrey last week, and a pickup band got formed to play it. Just a one-time gig with two folks from SunTex and a professor from Cornell. They played a few songs, and everyone had a grand time. But now the professor's gone, and the other two want to start a band. I'll be the singer." He fist-pumps the ceiling with both arms. "We've got a band again!"

I nod my approval. "Nice, Standard. Just you? What about Iggy and Boom?"

"Yeah, well the band already has a guitar and bass player, and they found a drummer at a different lab. All they needed was a singer, and the four of us had a great rehearsal last night."

"OK, who's in the band?"

Standard lists the band members. The guitarist is Banana Slug, properly known as Forrest Klein, an audio researcher at SunTex with long blond hair, a full beard, and an eternally wicked grin. He has a love/hate relationship with the garden pests and once tried to blend them and eat them but discovered he had to add equal parts of hot sauce to choke it down.

The bass player is also from SunTex and goes by the nickname, Prime, although he's really Bob Bullrun, a shy but brilliant digital currency specialist. Prime has dark wavy hair, a thin beard, wire-rim glasses, and the sly smile of someone with a secret.

The most surprising member of the band is the drummer, William Smart, who goes by the nickname, Tetris. Also bearded but mostly bald with a dark ring of former hair circling the sides, Tetris is well-known in the valley because he's the Chief Technology Officer of Park Ex, and he runs their lab with a staff of fifty researchers. He's a stocky man who takes his drumming as seriously as his science: carefully considered and whole-heartedly ventured. He got his nickname by writing a program to play the game of Tetris, which led him to conclude that the game is unwinnable because even his program, with instant and optimal decisions, eventually loses.

I congratulate Standard on his new band, and wish them well. He tells me they're playing a party at Blue's place in two weeks, and they're scrambling to get enough songs together. Then he unfolds himself from my chair and vaults from my office.

I'm at Blue's for the party, and as promised, Standard's there with the other three, making final adjustments to the equipment. Soon enough, they take their places, and Standard introduces the band.

"Hey everyone. We're Big Rig Pileup, and we're going to rock your heads off." As the music begins, I see something the old band never had: a light show. Mountain Dew, one of the researchers at SunTex, is working a bank of switches, bathing the performers in different color lights as they play, even occasionally torching a mirror ball that hangs from the ceiling. He's Henry Tack, a soda-fed man with a mustache and a penchant for drinking enough Mountain Dew to get hangovers the next day. The band is tight, and they play hard-driving tunes that shake the walls. Everyone has a fine time.

Over the next few months, Big Rig Pileup plays more and more shows. They do nerd parties, Halloween events, even a show at a San Francisco yacht club. And they've attracted more people to support them. Barry Spear, a researcher from our lab, has bought a fog machine and likes to fill each performance with piña colada-scented mist. Naturally, we call him Fog. His thin face sports no facial hair, which makes his smiles grow particularly wide when he's leaning on the control button to turn the air white.

There's even another member of the crew, Bentley, a researcher at Park Ex, who runs a sound board to support the band's increasingly complex noise-making. He's Ken Currant, a tall and solid man with thinning hair and the serious look of someone who needs to get the music right. Everyone calls him Bentley because he actually drives one of these super-luxurious cars, purchased used but lovingly restored.

Given the size of Big Rig Pileup and their crew, weekly rehearsals quickly turn into massive dinner parties where they get drunk and stoned, then concoct increasingly complex stunts. Mountain Dew acquires an endless array of lights, stands, mirrors, and switches. Fog gets a second fog machine and encourages the audience to control it, dropping the band into occasional moments of total opacity. And Bentley can't resist sound effects, layering tricks, and other audio abuse to make the music scintillate.

The band continues to search for new stunts and soon starts to engage in self-destructive ones. They insult themselves and their music at every opportunity and extend the distain to their audience, who they care about very little. They play on the streets of Palo Alto one evening, but the open guitar case that usually requests donations now has a sign inviting people to *take* some money. Before one of their shows, they distribute flyers announcing the performance, but every flyer lists a different band name. One flyer advertises The Creeping Features; another is for Box of Rocks; a third is for The Vampire Lestat; and a fourth promotes a show by NWA (Nerds With Attitudes). Each flyer advertises the same performance, so nobody knows for sure who they're coming to see.

At the end of one show, the band members turn their backs, bend over, and drop trow, joyfully mooning the audience. At another show, they stage a fight where Standard and Banana Slug go at it in mock viciousness, exchanging pulled punches, wielding rubber knives, and soaking themselves in stage blood. It's great entertainment, but is it music?

One night, performing in a small nightclub, they fill the space with so much fog the city Fire Marshall shuts them down. Each new stunt seems to delight the band, amaze the audience, and cement Big Rig Pileup's reputation as more of a Dada art group than a musical one.

Standard comes to my office one day, flush and practically delirious, his head spinning, mouth agog, hands shaking in the air. I usher him in then peek into the hall to make sure there aren't any cameras nearby. Nobody in the lab knows what antics they'll do next, and few want to be part of their sideshows.

"OK, Standard. What now?"

He practically shouts it out. "We've made it! Our stupid stunts haven't hurt our reputation, they've magnified it, and we've gotten noticed by the fame machine. The Rolling Stones want us to be their opening act. We're doing a show with them next month at the ball park in San Francisco, then we join the rest of the tour for six months. I can't believe it!"

I am impressed. "Congrats! Guess that proves it's more about the showmanship than the music." Honestly, the band's not bad. They're tight, and they deliver good songs, but they're not world-class. Andy Warhol promised everyone fifteen minutes of fame, and Big Rig Pileup is getting theirs.

But fame has a dark side that soon overshadows the thrill. Every few days, when Standard comes to my office, his mood is slightly worse. At first, he's concerned about spending six months on the road. He's in the middle of an interesting project, and it bothers him to leave it behind. The next time he shows up, he's annoyed by the PR people who've changed the band's name to something everyone in the group thinks is insipid. Then they want the band to spend days in a studio making better recordings. After that, they insist on giving the nerds makeovers with better haircuts, shaved beards, snappier outfits, and edgy accessories. But when they bring in a trainer and make the band start hours of daily exercise to get in better shape, Standard seems positively mortified. He's already losing sleep over this, and the extra time required by their sudden popularity is making life unacceptable.

Standard isn't the only one annoyed by fame. Tetris has a full lab under him, with managerial responsibilities that consume his attention. He's seriously peeved that his hobby has taken over his life. Prime is close to launching a digital payment scheme and needs to be available. Even Banana Slug is wary because he'd gladly chuck his computing career for a shot at fame, but he's no longer sure that being comic-relief for the Rolling Stones has any long-term potential. By the time the big arena show happens, none of the members of Big Rig Pileup are ready for their moment.

I'm in the audience that night, standing with Bentley. His sound work wasn't needed by the larger production team, so he's just a fan tonight and slightly grumpy about it. I point out that the band isn't totally jazzed to be up there, and he agrees that it's a problem. But he gives me a wink and tells me that he came up with an interesting idea that will solve everything. I ask about details, but he shakes his head and urges me to enjoy the show.

Big Rig Pileup takes the stage as the warm-up act, but the announcer uses their new name, Mo Mo Plate. I frown when I hear this, but Bentley just laughs. They play the songs with workman efficiency, plowing through each tune properly, musically, and unemotionally. But the songs are catchy, so the audience is as stoked as could be expected for an opening act. They finish their set and leave the stage.

Roadies crawl over the stage, disassembling Mo Mo Plate and setting up for the Stones. When they're done, the audience tension begins to build for the act they've paid dearly to see. Suddenly, Mo Mo Plate returns to the stage, picking up the guitars, microphones, and drumsticks of their famous partners. They reintroduce themselves as Big Rig Pileup and dive into one of their most enthusiastic songs. The audience is stoked, but the roadies are still onstage, staring at each other with confused looks and false starts in feeble attempts to control the chaos. Halfway through the song, the sound cuts out, but that doesn't stop Big Rig Pileup. They continue acoustically, Standard screaming songs so hard his voice rasps and cracks. When the song ends, security goons swarm the stage to pull the nerds away.

Big Rig Pileup concludes their six-month tour that night, and none of them misses a day of work.

About the Author

Steve Rubin has been programming since 1968 and still enjoys a few rounds with the keyboard. He's worked at many of the major research labs, from Bell Telephone Laboratories to Apple Computer with some startup work and plenty of consulting in between. Along the way, he made friends with every sort of nerd, since after all, he's one too.

Now retired, Rubin enjoys writing fiction and has penned a half-dozen romance novels using a pseudonym. He and his wife (another early computer nerd) have been happily married for over forty years and have raised two wonderful children. To escape the scourge of nerds, the couple recently fled Silicon Valley and now enjoy life in South Carolina. You can still find him talking about computers, but only if you take one of his home school or adult education classes.

Steve Rubin enjoys life so very much that he wouldn't trade places with anyone else, living or dead, real or imagined.